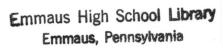

FIGHTING BACK

SUSAN KUKLIN

FIGHTING BACK

What some people are doing about AIDS

G. P. PUTNAM'S SONS • NEW YORK

for all the people who have AIDS or ARC,
those who stand beside them,
and for James A. Martin

Copyright © 1989 by Susan Kuklin. All rights reserved.
This book, or parts thereof, may not be reproduced.
in any form without permission in writing from the publisher.
Published simultaneously in Canada. Book design by Golda Laurens
Printed in the United States of America
Library of Congress Cataloging-in-Publication Data
Kuklin, Susan. Fighting back : what some people are
doing about AIDS/ Susan Kuklin. p. cm.
1. AIDS (Disease)—Social aspects. 2. Gay Men's Health Crisis, Inc.
3. AIDS (Disease)—Palliative treatment. I. Title.
RA644.A25K85 1988 362.1'969792—dc19 88-14906 CIP
ISBN 0-399-21621-9 First impression

CONTENTS

Team Seven

INTRODUCTION

Fighting Back reports the events of a nine-month period that I spent with a team of volunteers who offer support to people with AIDS in New York City. These volunteers serve in one of the divisions of Gay Men's Health Crisis (GMHC), an organization that was founded in 1981 by a group of gay men to confront the emergency caused by the AIDS epidemic.

The volunteers are called buddies. They assist clients who are persons with AIDS (Acquired Immune Deficiency Syndrome), or ARC (AIDS Related Complex), to regain control of their lives by, among other things, helping with their day-to-day chores. All persons with AIDS or ARC are eligible to be clients except ongoing drug abusers who are not in a detoxification program. In New York City this program is very large. There are so many volunteers that there is sometimes as much as a three- to four-month waiting list to become a buddy.

Candidates for buddy positions are screened to ensure that they have stable personalities and are committed to the program. GMHC does not explore a person's professional history or sexual orientation.

Training sessions, limited to sixty volunteers, take place every six weeks. I attended one of them. There were lectures by representatives of the different services offered by the organization: a doctor, a lawyer, a financial adviser, a psychologist. A client also spoke. A lot of factual information about AIDS, including how it is transmitted (insofar as this is

known), symptoms, treatment, etc. was given. I was surprised at how organized and upbeat everyone was, from Richard Dunne, the Executive
Director of GMHC, to a person with AIDS, who spoke candidly about his
illness.

We were taught how to work with a client, including the time require-
ments and the dos and don'ts. A buddy's work may be as mundane as
doing the laundry or picking up a meal. A client might be feeling well and
simply want to go out to a movie without any talk about AIDS. But if a
client in crisis calls, the buddy must be prepared to go. Confidentiality is of
extreme importance. Volunteers must pledge that they will not talk about
their clients outside the agency.

When we broke into small groups, we discussed many questions we
ourselves had raised. "Why are we doing this?" "What are we getting out
of it?" "What is going to scare us?" "What is going to challenge us?"

Joe Dolce, one of the buddies in this book, told me that before the
training, AIDS sounded like science fiction. "The Earthlings versus the
Martians, the latter being people with AIDS. The training made AIDS a
very human matter."

Once a volunteer is trained, he or she is assigned to a team. Between
twelve and twenty people make up a team, including a captain, nurse,
financial adviser, and secretary. Meetings are held every month, usually in
the early evening. The buddies report on their clients and share the latest
practical and medical information. Every time a buddy sees a client a report is written and filed at the GMHC's office. Because confidentiality is a
predominant interest of GMHC, these meetings serve as the primary place
buddies can vent their frustrations and apprehensions.

In order to show what it is like to be working with a potentially terminal illness, I interviewed and photographed those associated with one particular team, Team Seven, in the East Village on the Lower East Side in
Manhattan. I have used GMHC's guidelines and terminology. Therefore,
a person with AIDS is called a "PWA" or a "client," not a "patient" and
never a "victim." To ensure the privacy of the PWA, only first names of
clients are used at buddy meetings and in this book. When I wrote about a
client from the buddy's recollection or when a participant chose to be
anonymous for any reason, I have changed their name, place of birth,

profession, and identity. I indicate this with "name and identity changed" in parentheses the first time they are introduced.

Even before the training session, I was not worried about catching AIDS. What I was uneasy about, though, was how to approach a perfect stranger and ask extremely personal questions about their life, sexual practices, and death. Once I began working, I was surprised how comfortable I was with every person I interviewed. They made me comfortable. I became part of the team and the buddies would frequently call to help me wade through the avalanche of material that was often confusing and conflicting. At the meetings I gave my report on *the book* as if it was a living, breathing client for everyone to care about and nurture.

I am grateful to GMHC for its confidence in giving me unlimited access to the buddies and their meetings. Jeff Natter, the Associate Coordinator of the Crisis Intervention Service, was encouraging, creative, joyful. Each evening he leaves his job a happy, exhausted man, and the world is a better place because of him. Carl Morse, who originally suggested that I do a book about AIDS, provided me with valuable insights and information. He also steered me through the initial phases by introducing me to a team captain, David Weaver, who gave me a primer course on AIDS and the buddy program, and to Peter Carey, who introduced me to Brooke Alderson, a shining star in this book. Doctors Jeffrey Wallach and John Montana, and their staff, Renate Bongiorno and Margaret Baker, R.N., took time from their packed schedule, often late at night or early in the morning, to meet with me and review my material. My husband, Bailey, laughed with me through the fun parts and held my hand through the rough parts. My wise and understanding editor, Refna Wilkin, gave me wonderful suggestions and recommendations. Others deserving special mention are Peter Schjeldahl, Laura Silverstein, Helen Bates, Theodora Lurie, Dr. Barry Gingell and Golda Laurens.

As I interviewed various buddies a recurrent theme was that their client gave them much more than they gave in return. That holds true for me, too. I have learned much from this project, and I hope the lessons will be clear to the reader. This is a tale of living, living with the right priorities.

One who demonstrates this by word, deed, and example is Kachin Fry's client, Michael. When we met early on in this project, I thought he would be simply one of the many PWAs whom I would be interviewing. Michael quickly became central to this book and to me personally.

If a congressional medal of honor could be awarded for all bravery above and beyond the call, surely Michael, Jon, John, Steven, and Dennis would be recipients. Their courage and dignity is the motivation for the title, *Fighting Back*.

The members of Team Seven—an unlikely group if ever there was one—are made up of men and women from various walks of life, sexual orientations, and ages. Like everyone else, their lives center around work, family, and friends. Unlike everyone else, they take time from their own needs in order to help human beings who were not otherwise part of their daily lives. Here is a community of people doing something extraordinary. At times they appeared to me larger than life.

Although every buddy and client is special, I could not include them all in this book. I apologize to those who are not prominently featured.

Like the other members on the team, whenever I was stuck or had a problem, I called the co-captain, Brooke Alderson, and she fixed it. She is the spirit behind *Fighting Back* and its fairy godmother. Thank you Team Seven, it's an honor to know you.

Ernesto Austin	Ed Hartmann
James A. Baggett	Vicky Nott
Joe Dolce	Linda O'Keeffe
Oliver Einstein	Robert Krieger
Dave Fischer	Kathleen O'Farrell
David Fletcher	David Smith
Mike Frasch	Warren Wyss
Katsuko Kachin Fry	John and Hank
Beverly Gray	

1 · FIGHTING BACK

Michael arrived at the hospital with gifts for his lover, Juan—a stuffed Sylvester-the-cat and a red T-shirt that said *I love you*. Though Juan was still conscious he responded only to Michael. He didn't know anyone else. Juan held the stuffed cat tightly and no one could take it away from him. Juan was dying of AIDS.

Kachin Fry, a volunteer in the buddy program for GMHC, raced from work to the hospital every day. She felt she had to support Juan, who was her client, and Michael. Eventually, she realized that she too needed someone to support her. "I just couldn't handle Juan's dying alone," she said. She called the co-captain of her buddy team, Brooke Alderson, but Brooke, an actress, was out of town working on a film. Then Kachin called another team member, Sister Kathleen.

Kachin said, "My buddy, Juan, is Catholic. I'm concerned about his spiritual welfare and I'm worried about his friend, Michael, too. Could you help me out?" Sister Kathleen agreed to be there for them.

Juan was already unconscious when Sister Kathleen arrived. Michael was at his bedside. He looked up at her, then turned back to Juan, kissed him on the forehead, and went into the hall with Kathleen. She said to him, "This is a very difficult moment for you. I will take care of the wake and funeral arrangements if you want me to." He gratefully accepted.

That evening at 6:15 Juan died. Kathleen was in the room with Michael, a few friends, and Juan's mother and sister. Just before he died, Kathleen said, "Maybe we could say a few simple prayers."

Everyone held hands as they said the "Our Father" and the "Hail Mary." Kathleen recited a few passages from the Scriptures.

Then Kachin rushed in. She had come straight from work, afraid that she would be too late. A curtain was already around Juan's bed. As Kachin went behind to see him, Kathleen looked wistfully at the drawn curtain. "I felt so sad for her. It's not easy."

When Juan's family and friends were ready to leave the hospital at 8:30, the drizzle outside had become a downpour. Michael was the last one to leave.

Michael says, "I've seen the face of death. I saw it in the room with Juan. While Juan was in and out of a coma, I would squeeze his hand real tight. He would squeeze it back. I bent over and said, 'Juan, I love you. I'm here for you and I'll never leave you.' As difficult as it was for me, it was harder for him. I begged him to let go. I said, 'Juan, please, let go and be at peace and be happy. You will be very, very happy.'"

Sister Kathleen returned home exhausted, but she had barely fallen asleep when Michael called. He told her he wasn't feeling well. She said, "Michael, you've been under a lot of stress. Try to relax. Get a good night's sleep because tomorrow is going to be busy with the wake and everything else."

He called back a second time and said, "You know I feel really worse."

"Give me twenty minutes."

When Kathleen arrived at Michael's apartment, she thought that, all of a sudden, he looked so weak. They hailed a cab and went to the hospital emergency room.

After an hour Michael was diagnosed as having pneumonia in both lungs. He would have to stay in the hospital. Juan's wake was the following day and Michael told his doctors, John Montana and Jeffery Wallach, that he *had* to go to it. The doctors thought that he was too sick.

Michael said, "I'm leaving. I'm just going to walk out." Reluctantly, they agreed that he could attend the wake, but he had to return to the hospital that night. Because of Michael's pneumonia, his friend, Ray, who is a nurse, arranged for an oxygen tank to be available.

At one o'clock the next day, Ray and Kathleen took Michael to the funeral home. He was holding his own physically, but emotionally he was pretty shaky, and he cried a lot. Throughout the afternoon and into the evening Juan's family and many friends came to the wake.

Kachin wasn't doing well emotionally either. Juan's death overwhelmed her. She was so depressed that she couldn't even see Michael. First she had watched Juan die, and now Michael was sick too. She didn't go to the wake or to the funeral. She stayed in bed for three days. "I just couldn't get up," she said.

Sister Kathleen called to comfort her. Kathleen knew from first-hand experience how hard it was to deal with the wakes and funerals of young people. When she was suddenly called upon in this crisis, her heart had immediately gone out to Michael, Juan, and Kachin.

At eight o'clock that night Kathleen held a service. Before it began, Ray thought Michael needed oxygen. He put a screen around him in the corner of the funeral parlor and administered it. The service ended at nine.

Everyone at the wake urged Michael not to go to the funeral the next day. He went from the funeral home into the hospital, where he was diagnosed with full-blown AIDS. He couldn't make the funeral.

Because Juan's mother only speaks Spanish, Kathleen arranged for the funeral Mass in English and in Spanish. She accompanied the funeral party to the burial and said a prayer at the grave. In the evening she returned to the hospital to see Michael. Even though he wasn't her client, Kathleen visited him every other day.

Michael was being given a drug called pentamidine that was making him nauseous. He couldn't eat, and his temperature remained at 103 degrees. When Kathleen visited him, he wanted to get up and walk. She thought this was good but he edged as far as the end of the bed and couldn't go any farther because he was so weak.

After a few days Kachin called Michael in the hospital to see how he was holding up. Softly he answered, "Well, I'm still here. . . ."

When Michael first went into the hospital, he phoned his friends and family and they phoned him. Then, when he became too weak to get out of the bed, he took the phone off the hook.

Kachin was so depressed that she was unable to work, but she bounced back enough to visit Michael. She wanted to help him as much as she could.

"She's wonderful," says Sister Kathleen of Kachin. "She is a wonderful woman. Juan's dying took a toll on her."

When Kachin went to the hospital she took care of Michael. She even washed his hair while he was in his hospital bed. Michael says, "Not only did she do it, but she did it perfectly. It blew me away."

Kachin says, "I was glad I was able to be helpful. I had taken a special program given by the Red Cross on home nursing care for people with AIDS. When I took it, I was the worst student, and everyone made fun of me."

"But she turned out to be the best," Michael comments proudly.

Michael says, "It was odd how some members of the hospital staff treated me. They seemed afraid of me. A few came into my room dressed in plastic gowns wearing gloves, goggles, and masks. At times I would look up at them in their space suits and think to myself, I must be on Mars.

"One guy wanted me to wear a mask when he took me to the X ray room. I swore at him. Let him put on a mask. If I had TB, no one would have thought twice about it, and that's much easier to catch than AIDS. I can understand someone putting gloves on when they draw blood. That makes perfect sense. I can also understand them putting on a mask because they didn't want to give me germs. For the most part, however, the hospital staff was wonderful to me."

Kachin saw Michael regularly. Many people visited, but Kachin felt they did not understand how much rest he needed. They came and they stayed and they talked. Michael liked it. When Kachin arrived, friends would leave them alone. She urged him to tell his friends that he was tired and needed to rest.

After two and a half weeks, Michael began recovering. He attributes his recovery to his friends and family as well as to his medication. "There were friends who came to see me in the hospital who really didn't think I was going to come out. At times I didn't think I was going to come out. Even though my friends didn't believe it, they would look at me and say, 'Don't worry. Everything is going to be okay. Don't worry.'"

*　　*　　*

Michael remembered how he first got sick. Six months after Juan was diagnosed as having AIDS, Michael became tired easily and ran high fevers. "I was drained and exhausted," he says. "I knew the chances were that I would test positive for the AIDS virus because I took part in a lot of promiscuous sex."

Michael went to the doctor and was diagnosed with ARC, AIDS-related complex. "I'm not going to feel sorry for myself because what's done is done. Now is important. Right now. Not tomorrow, not yesterday."

Michael's friends begged him to take it easy. But he continued working and went to the hospital every night to see Juan. "No matter how I felt, I was not going to let him go through it alone. I borrowed money. I took taxis. Here was the love of my life dying, and there was no way I was not going to be there for him. I'm not complaining about it. I would have done twice as much."

Juan's financial situation was getting serious. He didn't have a job before he was diagnosed, therefore he wasn't covered by medical insurance. Some of Juan's expenses were covered by Medicaid, but Michael couldn't afford to pay Juan's enormous additional medical bills.

Kachin called Ernesto Austin, a financial adviser for Team Seven, to find out what emergency loans were available.

Michael was somewhat luckier with his own finances. His company was very understanding, and his boss said he could work a couple of days a week, so Michael was covered by insurance.

But money was getting tight for both Juan and Michael. They couldn't even afford their huge laundry bills.

Kachin knew from the education program at GMHC that she could not catch the disease from doing laundry, and she wanted to find a way to ease their financial burden. She asked Brooke's help. Brooke has a washer-dryer in her apartment, and she, her husband, and nine-year-old daughter offered to go to Juan and Michael's apartment, which was down the street, to pick up laundry every few days, do it, and return it.

Kachin called constantly and talked with Michael. Juan, who had always been extremely shy, never spoke to anyone except Michael.

One topic Michael and Juan didn't discuss was AIDS. The only allusion to it was when Michael checked that Juan had taken his medication.

Eventually Juan changed and he began talking. Kachin, surprised to hear his voice, knew something different was going on.

Once, when Kachin was visiting Juan while Michael was at work, he talked on and on, so fast she could hardly understand him.

As Juan's condition worsened, Michael saw it, but he couldn't talk about it to anybody. He kept saying, "I hope Juan gets better and better." Kachin suggested that he ask Juan what he wanted most. When he asked, Juan told him he wanted to go to the country. Everyone, including Juan, knew that was impossible. Michael brought in a pile of photographs of the two of them in the country when they were healthy.

Juan finally talked about the inevitable. He told Michael that he wanted to be placed on a life-support system. This never became necessary.

2 · TEAM SEVEN

WHOMP!!! A large beige rabbit landed in the middle of a plate of cookies overturning a bowl of ice cubes. "Grab the soda!" someone shouted. "Be careful, there goes the wine and chips," called another.

"Ginger. No!" said Brooke, using her most awesome theater voice. Ginger, the rabbit, ran off chasing the two family cats. Team Seven was meeting as usual at Brooke's apartment.

Warren Wyss, the co-captain, read announcements of upcoming events sponsored by GMHC. Mike Frasch, the team's nurse, described the latest medical news and research. The team secretary wrote furiously, trying to catch every word.

Then the team members reported on their clients' status. James Baggett, the youngest member of the team, began by saying that his new referral, Jon (name and identity changed), was a thirty-year-old actor who was recently diagnosed with PCP, *pneumocystis carinii pneumonia,* an opportunistic infection. All of us have the protozoan organism, pneumocystis, in our lungs but only severely immune suppressed persons are susceptible to PCP. This week he was telling his family about his condition. Jon had initially developed side effects from AZT, a drug he's taking, that has had some success in slowing down the virus. He was now feeling well and didn't need a buddy to help out with household chores. What he did need was someone he could talk to freely about his illness, who would share an occasional movie, or go to dinner. James was happy to do that.

Kachin was at work styling a fashion photography session, but she had called in her monthly progress report about Juan and Michael. Brooke told the rest of the team about Juan's death and Michael's hospitalization. They were very upset. Losing a client, even one they had never met, was tough, and Juan and Michael were particular favorites of the team. They were saddened by the news, and they were also concerned for Kachin because Juan and Michael were like family to her.

Linda O'Keeffe, an Englishwoman who writes, edits, and designs a column for a major newspaper, spoke next. Her buddy, David (name and identity changed), had also died. His vital signs dropped and he refused medication, fell into a coma, and died peacefully.

Linda, always candid with her feelings, confided that David had driven her nuts, and that at times she felt guilty and didn't want to see him. That increased her guilt. She felt useless and incapable. She asked if others ever had these feelings.

"Do you feel old?" James Baggett looked toward Linda. "At twenty-six I've seen so many people die that I feel old."

Linda pondered James's remark and nodded in agreement. Despite his youth, James played a prominent role at the meetings. He had already spent three years on another team and had had numerous clients. He had often experienced what the rookie members were now feeling. Sharing these reactions and emotions was a vital part of these meetings.

Brooke suggested that one couldn't always predict the repercussions of a client passing away. She continued, "It is difficult—more often for men than for women—to talk about emotions. Women often verbalize their feelings better than men."

Robert Krieger, another team member, raised his hand. "I call for a vote to decide if this is a sexist remark."

"Yea," shouted all the men, laughing.

The women hissed and Brooke roared with laughter. Everyone relaxed.

Linda O'Keeffe

It has always been important for Linda to understand the motivations for her actions. She believes that she became a buddy for selfish reasons. She says, "I became interested in GMHC when a friend of mine came down with AIDS and died. I didn't know how to handle it. The way I reacted was with anger, mixed with fear, and frustration, and feelings of absolute futility and hopelessness. It was horrible. Also, I never felt that I did enough to help my friend. That was the worst part of it. I thought, I can't go through this again. I have to do something positive. GMHC seemed the perfect organization because it would allow me to constructively help someone."

A week after the training program, Linda was assigned to David. She was scared. Their first meeting was in the hospital. She says, "I went toward his room and I thought I was going to throw up. I saw him through the crack in the door and I ran. I called a friend. My friend wasn't home. I thought, oh God, what am I going to do?"

David was 50 years old and a successful lawyer. He had cytomegalovirus (CMV), which attacks various organs of the body and often leads to blindness, dementia, and death. When Linda met him he was partially blind, and he could barely make out what she looked like. He was to become totally blind within a few weeks.

Linda had to make herself go through the door. David's mother and sister were in the room and she didn't know what they knew. Should she say, "Hi, I'm Linda O'Keeffe from GMHC?" What if they asked, "What's GMHC?" What if they didn't know that David had AIDS? Fortunately, it turned out that the family knew everything and was very supportive.

David initially specified that he wanted a woman buddy. During their first meeting he told Linda he wanted a woman because he didn't feel at ease asking a man to do household chores. That didn't go down too well with her, but she gritted her teeth and made a joke of it. She said, "Well, I don't do windows." That broke the ice.

Later David said that he didn't want a woman buddy, he wanted a man. He was going through a stage, not uncommon among AIDS patients, in which he kept changing his mind. Possibly this was a way of keeping control of his life. Finally he accepted Linda and she began visiting him regularly.

"My main function was to read," Linda says. "David told me that once his friends knew that he had AIDS, not one person walked into his apart-

Linda

ment or called up without giving him advice. They told him what he should do, how he should eat, what he should wear, what he should take. He was fed up with advice." Linda promised herself that she was going to do what he wanted. No suggestions. She would let him call the shots.

"One of the most difficult things for me to deal with in the AIDS work was the feeling that I was not accomplishing anything. My natural tendency is to come into a situation and say, okay, let's get this organized: we'll do this, and we'll do that. My tendency is to *do*. I'm a doer. Doing is how I unload my emotions: the pent-up anger, the frustrations, whatever. The hardest part of my work with David was to realize that I couldn't really do anything." The practical elements were all in place: friends and family helped with meals and laundry. He was financially secure. No one could change the fact that he had AIDS.

"I can't say that I was particularly close to David. We never had long, involved conversations. We weren't friends in the traditional sense. Because he was dying, the six months we knew each other had a new intensity for me."

When it became clear that David was within a few weeks of the end, Linda began to experience emotions that she couldn't deal with. She found she hated to visit him. She never knew what to expect. Would he be totally passive, or screaming? She talked at length to Brooke about it.

"I questioned the point of going to see him at all. I was frightened that David was going to ask me questions that I didn't know how to answer. I needed a strong support system from my friends."

Although many of Linda's friends are gay, she had the greatest difficulty talking to them about AIDS. "It's too close for them. Too unnerving. I find that the people who can help me the most are those who are working with PWAs."

David had a nurse round the clock, but he wanted to be left alone to die. He would shout about the injustice of his condition and about the pain he was in. Linda might walk into David's apartment to find him screaming that he wanted to die, and for her to get out. She tried not to take it personally, but of course she did. "I felt anger, frustration, intense sadness—exactly the way I felt when my friend died."

People tell Linda she is doing such wonderful work, but she doesn't see it in those terms. Linda says, "It might sound strange but when I was with David I would think what an amazing person this is. His strength devastated me at times. The fact that he often had a sense of humor, despite his intense pain, was extraordinary. Many times I came away from him thinking, my God—just to be with him is a privilege. I'm always in touch with what I'm getting out of my experiences. By going through this with David, I found that I could deal with AIDS."

James A. Baggett

James says that there are three things straight people assume when they learn that someone is gay: He is promiscuous, he is attracted to *any* male, and he has been exposed to the virus. James is gay, and yet none of the above apply to him. Coming of age in the age of AIDS has made James very cautious. "Because I have never had unsafe sex, many think of me as being a real prude.

"I grew up with the last name Baggett which was one step away from faggot." The kids were quick with the nickname and teased him horribly. At first, he tried to be as macho as possible, but he found that became exhausting. By the time he was in the 9th or 10th grade, he decided that putting on a front was unimportant. People would either like him or not. More important was that *he* must be his own self. "When I realized this, I became a happier person.

"The gay kids I knew in school were the best little boys. We were proper, 'A' students who would never be the ones to break windows. For some reason we were always trying to live up to other people's expectations."

James's father is a business executive and his mother works in a gift shop in his hometown, St. Louis. They always did volunteer work. "I was raised with the understanding that you should help others. When I wanted to be a veterinarian, I worked at the Humane Society. I feel strongly about compassion and conviction."

Now that James has left his hometown and lives in New York City, his life is considerably different from that of the young boy who was tormented because his name was Baggett. As an editor and film critic he leads a glamorous life. He is invited to Broadway openings, film screenings, the latest dance clubs. He has many good friends, straight and gay, and he is always busy.

Still, James has not forgotten the lessons he learned in St. Louis. True to his history of helping others, when he became an editor of a trendy magazine for teens, he started a writing program for gifted inner-city kids.

"Living here in the City makes it easy to become self-absorbed. Helping people who are needy puts my life into perspective. I get out of myself and avoid dwelling on my own problems. Although I love the glitz, I don't want to take it too seriously."

There is another side to his life besides glamour. James is surrounded by AIDS. "I work with people who have AIDS and I have friends who have

James

AIDS. When I'm with my friends we sometimes vow that we will go through the day without mentioning The Word. We call it the 'A-word.' No matter what, it comes up."

When James volunteered to be a buddy for GMHC, his first client was a Venezuelan who didn't speak English. The second one only wanted to listen to music and smoke pot. The third was so sick he couldn't even talk. The fourth was bossy and nasty. Then he was assigned to a city planner with a degree in English literature. This was the first client James really liked. They had much in common, and when he died, James took his death hard. His work began to suffer. He had seen too much sickness, too many deaths. He was burnt out.

James did not immediately take another client. He went to Europe and, relieved to be away from AIDS and all its stresses, vowed not to do any more work as a buddy.

When James returned from Europe there was a message on his machine from Jeff Natter, the assistant head of the volunteers for GMHC. An actor needed a buddy, and Jeff, who makes client referrals, thought he would be a good client for James. James admired Jeff so much that he could not refuse.

James and his new client, Jon, liked one another immediately. They felt as if they had been tight friends all their lives. Jon accompanies James to film screenings and theater openings, while James sits in on Jon's acting workshops and meets his famous colleagues. "It's wonderful going around town with Jon because he knows *everything* about *everybody*. He's up on the latest dirt and I love to dish theater gossip."

One thing that is never gossiped about is the fact that Jon has AIDS. No one in New York knows except James, Jon's doctors, his roommate, and GMHC.

James's Client, Jon

Before Jon was diagnosed, he had called his mother to tell her about a friend from their town who recently died of AIDS. His mother's first reaction was, "What a thing to bring home to a mother."

"I got really pissed. What about him? What about what *he* had to come home to? What did he do wrong? Nothing. He got sick."

Last summer Jon was in an off-Broadway show in which he played a very demanding role. When he noticed that he had lost ten pounds, he thought it was because he was working so hard. In another few days he lost five pounds more. He knew something was wrong, but decided not to think about it until the show closed.

Jon's mother and sister flew in from the Midwest to see the last Saturday matinee. They were worried that he looked so thin. They left that night and the next morning he awoke with a fever of 102. There was another matinee performance on Sunday. The stage manager had to practically push Jon on stage. In between acts, he washed himself in cold water to keep his fever down. Somehow he got through the performance, went home, and collapsed.

The next day Jon was tested for AIDS. Although he had a mild case of pneumonia, he didn't have to go to the hospital. He lay in bed at home for two weeks and lost another fifteen pounds. When the tests came back positive, he called GMHC and asked for a buddy.

"I lay in bed thinking that I could not tell my family over the phone. When they called every Sunday, I would hang over the side of the bed in agony while cheerfully acting like nothing was wrong. 'Hi . . . Oh, I'm fine . . .'"

The entire time Jon lay in bed, he kept hearing his mother's voice, "What a thing to bring home to a mother." It obsessed him. He had heard all sorts of awful stories of what happened when a person told his family he had AIDS. Although his family knew that he was gay, they never actually talked about it. He didn't think his family would hate him or disown him, but he knew that even if there were only snide comments, it would tear him apart. He worried about his brother-in-law who was very macho. Would he allow Jon to be with his niece and nephew?

Throughout July Jon forced himself to eat. By August he appeared fairly healthy. He wanted to tell his family he had AIDS without shocking them by his physical appearance.

When Jon finally went home, he let a few days go by without saying anything because he didn't want to ruin their happy reunion. "Finally I said to my mother and sister, 'Let's go for a ride, *now.*' The kids wanted to come, but I said no. My sister knew something was up.

"We went for a drive and I tried to talk, but all I could do was cry. I couldn't get the words out. I was so emotional, they freaked out."

Jon told his mother and sister that he had lost a lot of weight, was very sick, and almost died. He said he had pneumonia and that it was AIDS related. "I could tell by the expressions on their faces that they thought that I was jumping to conclusions. They wrote the whole thing off as 'Jon's being dramatic again.' "

He pressed on about how fearful he was that his brother-in-law would keep the children away from him. At the height of his emotions, he began ranting and raving at how little this country did to fight AIDS. Jon's mother, who was very patriotic, didn't like that at all. She became very upset.

"Mostly they were shocked and silent. My sister said she was only concerned for me. My mother became a rock and stared into space. She thought she was being strong, but I could see doors slamming shut. Years ago she had lost one daughter in a car accident and last year my father died of a heart attack. And now . . . What a thing to bring home to a mother . . .

"For the rest of the vacation, nothing was said. That is typical of my Irish Catholic upbringing: show no emotions, stifle everything."

Jon didn't know until later that his sister had told her husband. Jon was afraid of his brother-in-law's reaction but he was wrong. His brother-in-law became very supportive and showed no "AIDS-phobia."

The family continues to call Jon every Sunday. All they want to hear is, "How do you feel?"

"I feel good."

"Fine."

"That's it. Someday I'd like to say that I am gay and we must talk about it.

"Ever since we were little, my sister always complained when I got something that she didn't. My mother told my sister that if anything happened to me, 'I'm going down "old glory road" with him.' 'Old glory road'? Can you believe it? I laughed when my mother told me this and asked her what my sister said. My sister, forgetting that she needn't get *everything* I get, hollered, 'What about me?'

"My mother has this romantic notion about us going down 'old glory road' together. She can't talk to me directly, yet I don't think she can bear losing me."

Katsuko Kachin Fry

Kachin is from Osaka, the second largest city in Japan. Her mother was a hairdresser, and her father ran a bakery. Kachin says, "I went to a very good school. We studied hard and competed in a lot of sports. We had to jog for hours. I thought, what's the point? My family expected me to get married to some nice rich man, but I had other ideas."

Kachin

Kachin left home and country when she was eighteen. "I was fascinated with America. I left my family and I moved to California because I wanted to live in a warm country with a nice beach. I dreamed about it when I was young. But I found that I didn't like the beach life. I grew up in a city with four seasons and I prefer that."

When Kachin arrived in the States she didn't understand English. "I took English grammar in school, but it was different from the spoken language. I couldn't even read a menu. I didn't understand the difference between bacon and avocado."

Kachin's first American job was as a waitress in a Japanese restaurant. She tried to talk with Americans and outside of work she didn't spend time with any Japanese people. She felt that she never fit into Japanese society.

In California she soon learned English and went to work for a textile designer. Although moving to America was a positive experience, Kachin was unhappy. "I never loved myself. I never felt that life was wonderful. I was very negative. In fact, I wanted to die."

Kachin came to New York, enrolled at the Fashion Institute of Technology, and took classes in sewing and dyeing. Once she learned draping, she began designing textiles and clothing for fashion designers and working as a stylist for high-fashion photographers. Still, she felt her life was empty.

In 1983 Kachin got married, but the marriage lasted only six months. After her separation she needed to do something in addition to work, and she wanted it to have some value. Kachin had heard of AIDS, but thought of it as a gay men's disease. When a friend died of it, she realized that the disease was going to destroy a lot of people. She wanted to understand more about AIDS, and help out.

Kachin says, "I don't like it when society discriminates. We all look different, and we grow up with different beliefs and ideas. Why have weird thoughts about gays and lesbians? I get angry at that.

"It is hard to meet new people," Kachin says blushing. "Having an affair is even harder. When I do spend time with someone I like a lot, before I even consider having an affair, I think, might he be HIV positive? Could *I* be positive?

"It is difficult to bring up the subject. But I know that I must. I say, 'You know what I do? I'm a volunteer for AIDS. I'm really educated about it. Do you ever think about AIDS? Don't you ever worry?' I carry a condom myself—just in case."

Volunteering to be a buddy changed Kachin's life. She says, "Before, I had lots of personal problems. I was often unhappy. One minute I could be up and the next I could be down. People didn't notice it since I can push myself to be friendly even when I'm depressed. After I met people with AIDS, I saw that life must have value. Here are people who are trying so hard to live. They have everything wrong with them, and every part of their bodies is in pain. But they still want to live, even in pain. Seeing that changed me around completely. Now I realize how meaningful and important life is. I'm growing up."

Michael

3 · AT WAR

The day Michael left the hospital, he stopped at the marketing firm on Park Avenue where he worked. He went into the president's office to thank him for the firm's continued support throughout his illness. Colleagues had visited him in the hospital, and the company insurance paid his medical bills. Michael was told he could return to work whenever he wished. He realized that people cared about him.

Once home Michael felt weak, and by the time he had climbed up the five flights to his apartment, he was utterly exhausted. When he opened the door, he found himself alone in the apartment for the first time since Juan died. Juan's clothing and personal belongings were everywhere.

Michael told himself that he must get rid of these things, and he also thought, "I took care of Juan for two years. Now I have to take care of myself. Now that comes first."

He called a department store and ordered a set of designer sheets. Never before one to run up bills for luxuries he could not afford, he was no longer willing to wait.

He says, "I'm tired of reading in the newspapers about the deaths of so many people. I'm tired of hearing on TV about the predictions that so many people will die. Numbers don't mean anything. It's the individual who counts. People survive all the time. And who knows, if scientists discovered penicillin from a piece of moldy bread, they might find a cure for AIDS tomorrow. *Don't tell me I'm going to die.* Every time I hear about the PWAs, I hear *'the victims, the victims.'* I'm not a victim. I'm living with an illness. I'm living with one, I'm not dying with one. I wish people would get it together about this. If I had strength, I'd call up every time I read about the 'victims' in the paper. Some people do make these calls and that's wonderful. Constantly hearing all the negatives about AIDS depresses me. It makes me feel that I am destined to die, and that takes the fight out of me. That's not fair. It's very wrong."

Michael is angry at the government, too. He believes, as many others do, that if the disease had affected mainly heterosexuals, much more would have been done. "As long as the people in power don't look at this disease as an epidemic that affects *everybody,* nothing's going to happen. That's victimizing. That's telling me that I'm a person no one cares about. Well, I don't care about them. I sound angry, but I'm not really angry. I'm being realistic. I'm not sitting back and accepting my fate. I know that I have to go on. And I'm going on, despite what anyone tells me."

Michael spent the first week out of the hospital trying to build up his strength. He was frustrated by his weakness. The first few days he tried to do too much. Kachin told him he had to learn how to relax. He knew that, but he couldn't do it.

He was taking a lot of medication, and some medicines counteracted other ones. One dulled his taste. "I might as well be eating chicken rather than yoghurt," he told his friends when they came around with health and gourmet foods and ice cream sodas.

The medication and the weakness were bad enough, but the worst pain came from the fact that Juan had died.

Juan and Michael were like any other couple. They had their difficulties and they fought, but their life together was happy. Michael says, "We lived together for eleven years. That's not peanuts, I'll tell you. We were both very quiet. He had his hobbies, I had mine. He loved bingo while I collected videos.

"When Juan was first rushed to the hospital, the attendants said his was one of the most difficult cases they had seen. He fought hard. He was very brave."

Michael knew that in order to fight AIDS, he had to regain his positive attitude. He searched for the good in his life. He notes, "GMHC has been great. The buddies are fabulous. Kachin is unbelievable. Brooke lives up the street and she has been doing my laundry. Her husband and daughter help out. Sister Kathleen gives me communion. Everybody is helping.

"What can I say? There are not enough people to help. There's not enough of anything. The ones who are here are doing a damn good job, and if it weren't for them, I would have no place to go. GMHC has a recreation center and now that I'm feeling a little better, I just hang out there for the most part. I meet people, sit in the office, and I've even joined an art group. I love that. I'm doing watercolors, and some people say I'm pretty good. I was there all day today and I'm going back tomorrow. What else am I going to do? Sit home?"

Another way Michael thought he could help himself fight AIDS is to help others, especially young people who are just beginning to discover their sexuality. Michael himself is now terrified about sex. He has totally lost interest in it and only thinks about staying healthy. "I want to inform people that they have to be sexually cautious. People must be damn sure they know who they are sleeping with. They must be sure that their partners are truthful about how many other people they've slept with. Promiscuous sex can be very dangerous. Unsafe sex is out. Definitely! Positively! Heterosexual, homosexual, whatever. Out! Period. There's no longer a choice about that. If a person does choose to have sex, the most important thing is to have safe sex. Use condoms. I would even be careful with condoms."

Brooke

4 · MORE BUDDIES

Brooke Alderson, Team Co-captain

The captain of a team acts as a liaison between the buddies and GMHC, leads the meetings, and acts as a back up if a buddy can't be there for a client. Brooke prefers to be available to many people rather than concentrating on one person.

"I approach AIDS with a war mentality. Here are young people dying in large numbers just like young men and women who go off to war. What's the difference?

"I also believe that whether one is fighting and dying on the front lines or home planting victory gardens, everyone is part of the war. Even people who deny this particular war and say it doesn't affect them, they are involved, too."

Brooke was watching a news program on TV one night when she saw a spot about a group of mothers in Queens who were protesting in front of a school. They were afraid that a child who tested HIV positive, which simply meant he had been infected with the HIV virus and is susceptible to AIDS, might be admitted to their neighborhood school. They didn't even know for sure that their school would have the student because students' records are confidential.

"It was the most grotesque thing I had ever seen," Brooke says. "The mothers made cardboard coffins on their strollers. They had their infant children sitting in the coffin-strollers. I thought it was too horrible. I am married and have a child. I didn't want my daughter growing up with only this as a model of how to deal with a crisis. I want her to be educated and to be part of the world. The demonstration is part of the world, unfortunately, but it is not the only part. The day after I saw that TV spot, I went to GMHC and volunteered."

Brooke's first client was Nicholas (name and identity changed). He put her through the roughest six months of her life. He was suffering minor dementia that manifested itself in many unanticipated ways. When she visited him, Brooke never knew what she was going to be asked to do or what condition he would be in.

As Nicholas's disease progressed, he became more and more bizarre. At one point he told Brooke that AIDS was a result of people killing whales. Brooke says, "Here I am, a wife and working mother, sitting by the bedside of a strange man talking about whales and I'm going, 'Oh, the whales . . .'"

Every day when Brooke arrived for her visit, Nicholas would be rearranging his furniture. Finally, his mother came from Italy to take him back to Florence where he died. Brooke says, "It was totally horrible. I last saw him about a week before he left and, believe me, I was ready for him to leave. There was continual emotional chaos around him that I was not prepared for.

"But in all fairness, Nicholas had an incredible spirit and will to live. He was resolute in his determination to beat AIDS. He died with his boots on. He was a remarkable person."

After Nicholas died, Brooke was a buddy to Jim and then to Jack (names changed). "I still miss Jack. He was a wonderful man. I really didn't want another person after Jack." She needed a break, and when Warren, the leader of Team Seven, was going out of town, he asked her to be co-captain. During that time another PWA needed a buddy and no one was available. "I took care of him, but my heart wasn't in it."

Every buddy has his or her own way of dealing with a client. Brooke focuses on the practical needs of the person. She does not linger on her own feelings. She says, "I become very involved in getting as much support for the clients as possible. I try to rally and coordinate friends, family, home, or hospital care. I make sure their nurses are there. It's more or less busy work and that helps me cope with it. I concentrate on their living."

Joe Dolce

Joe, a free-lance writer, was having lunch with an old friend from high school in New Jersey, when she told him she had become a buddy. "She wasn't gay. She had a lot of gay friends, but who doesn't in New York. I thought it was pretty amazing that she was involved, when AIDS was less in her reality than it is in mine."

Joe hesitated before calling GMHC. He says, "I was afraid of AIDS. I was a victim of fear because I didn't understand the disease although, being gay myself, I thought I was at risk of getting it. I'm thirty years old and I've learned that the only way I can deal with fear is to confront it or run away from it. Since there was no place to run, I decided I might as well confront it."

Joe did not want to offer his skills as a writer and publicist to GMHC. He said no to administrative work and no to political work. "I wanted to deal with the human experience of AIDS. I needed to see it in terms of a human problem. I wanted to involve my being."

Once Joe was assigned to Team Seven he immediately got a client, Anthony (name and identity changed). After all the hours of training, Joe still felt unprepared. He knew he had to rely on his own choices, his own wits. His approach was, "You have AIDS. I don't. I am not a martyr. I have no desire to be a martyr. I'm here for a selfish reason, to find out about this disease. I'll help you any way I can."

Anthony's reply was, "Oh, thank God, you're not a Florence Nightingale type."

Joe told his client, "I have a life. I have a schedule. I'll be here for you when I can. I can't be a nurse." Anthony didn't want a nurse, and so a friendship began.

For Joe it was a wonderful beginning because Anthony and he shared similar tastes in food. Anthony was a vegetarian and Joe doesn't eat red meat. Joe is a good cook, although he never cooks for himself, so he went to Anthony's apartment two or three times a week, cooked, and then they had dinner together. "That was more than I originally planned to do. But I liked him so much.

"Anthony was an architect whose lover had recently died of AIDS. He was probably very handsome when he was well, but when I came on he was pretty skinny. So I was involved—more involved than I anticipated."

Anthony became worried because he was rapidly losing weight, so he checked himself into the hospital. Like Linda's client, David, he had cytomegalovirus (CMV) and it was beginning to affect his vision. To avoid blindness and dementia a drug was administered three times a week by a catheter, called a Hickman catheter, that was permanently installed in his chest. The drug, however, lowers the white blood cell count. Anthony hated chemicals in general and he hated the treatment because it made his food taste like rust. After a while he refused to continue with it.

At the time, Joe was out of town on a writing assignment, but he heard what happened. "Shortly after the catheter was removed, Anthony started to go crazy, but in a great way. He did it with flair. One night, armed with cab fare and department store charge cards, he wrapped himself in a sheet and broke out of the hospital. Tall as he was, he must have weighed about 120 pounds. He looked like Gandhi. He went to Barney's, an exclusive department store, and selected seven suits. He got as far as the register to charge them before the manager noticed that something was not quite right. Who was this skinny man wrapped in a sheet, wearing a hospital band? The manager called the hospital.

"When I returned from my trip, Anthony's business partner, Helen (name changed), told me about the adventure. I called him. 'Heard you've been shopping, Tony.' 'Seven Perry Ellis suits for $1400. That was a deal,' he told me. He knew I loved bargains."

In the weeks following, Anthony became more deranged. Most of his friends couldn't deal with him. Joe says, "It was basically Helen, his

Joe

brother-in-law, and I who were there for him. His sister couldn't walk in the door without breaking down and crying. His brother wouldn't let Anthony into his house, for fear he would contaminate his kids. His parents were dead. Anthony's brother-in-law was his financial adviser. He was good at that, but terrible about household things. He once washed all of Anthony's imported wool sweaters in hot water. They shrank to nothing. Domestically, he was utterly useless—a useless straight man who couldn't even do his own wash. Anthony got pretty pissed off."

"What's it like to be dying?" Joe once asked Anthony while they were sharing a meal. Joe says, "Anthony was interested in talking about it. What concerned him most was not the physical part. He had been through so much pain by the time I got there. He wasn't afraid of death. Total loss of control was more difficult for him than the pain. I think the inability to control his life had a lot to do with his shopping spree. For an instant he needed to take charge of his life and to convince himself that he wasn't dying. But of all things . . . business suits!"

When Anthony's health declined further, he was moved into a hospice that had an attractive private room with nursing care readily available. While there he became completely demented and needed sedation. Joe knew Anthony was going to die soon, and to prepare himself, he had long talks with Anthony's partner, Helen.

They became close friends. Joe says, "We were on the phone at all times of the night. Her husband must have gone crazy. We'd call each other at six in the morning, at two in the morning. The hour never mattered. We couldn't stop talking about it."

The other person who greatly helped Joe was John Montana, who was also Michael's doctor. Joe says, "Dr. Montana is an archangel. He said we could call him at any hour, and we did. We called about everything. 'Can Anthony take aspirin?' 'Is the dose of the pain-killer strong enough?' Dr. Montana carefully explained what was happening. We must have driven him crazy. I guess we were driving everybody crazy."

Joe and Helen rotated their visits so that one of them was there every night. A full-time nurse was on duty, but they wanted to make sure Anthony was comfortable.

Joe once found the nurse hiding in the closet. Anthony had told her to get out, but she wouldn't leave him alone.

People don't die of AIDS itself. They die of the opportunistic infections that flourish when AIDS destroys the immune system. "Opportune" means the infection takes advantage of the weakened defenses and does its dirty work. Joe and Helen had no idea of what half Anthony's infections were. They watched his temperature go from 105 degrees to 99 within half an hour. Was that normal for a person with AIDS? Was it temporary? Was it due to all the drugs he was taking?

Joe says, "It was awful. I thought, what's going on here, this guy is thirty-five years old, how can he be dying? I walked down the street crying, which was amazing because in my family boys don't cry."

It became a very intense experience for Joe to support someone who was going through one of the peak moments in life—death.

Joe says, "The act of giving of yourself without expectation or ego is a profound one. It changed me. After Anthony died, I didn't take a client. I began working on some stories. Emotionally, I was haunted by Anthony."

Beverly Gray

Beverly, who was born and raised in London, left school when she was sixteen. She was a punk rocker. "I thought hairdressing would be a great profession," she says. "I could go to work with my hair purple and I could dress whatever way I wanted to. I was being creative. It was one of those jobs that was a very trendy thing to do at that time, and I was very trendy."

Beverly

Outwardly, Beverly appeared self-assured and together, but inside, she was shy and fragile. She says, "I was intimidated by men chatting me up. Though I am straight, I never felt comfortable when a boy would ask me to dance or try to kiss me."

Beverly met Stephen in London. They lived together as best friends even though he is gay. Stephen moved to the States to open a beauty salon. After three months, he asked her to join him. Stephen wanted them to get married. She said, "Why not?"

Beverly's parents, who knew he was gay, were quite upset about the marriage. Beverly says, "Stephen is very eccentric. I suppose I am, too, to a certain extent. I thought, why shouldn't we get married? We love each other. We care for each other. I'm straight. He's gay. Who cares? We had a great wedding. Our families came. Stephen wore a pink suit, I had pink hair. It was a very camp wedding, and everyone loved it. We were young and doing what we wanted to do."

Last year the lover of a good friend of Beverly's died of AIDS. Though she didn't know the lover well, she was a support person for her friend. Other friends were dropping out of their lives. Beverly thought, What's going on? Why did they leave? "I became a much stronger person because I was helping someone. I'm twenty-six, and I'd never been supportive to anyone. I've always been scared about sickness and death. Yet here I was in a situation where a friend of mine needed me. How could I possibly not be there? Once I saw how helpful I could be to my friend, I wanted to do more."

Beverly decided to call GMHC. Everyone told her not to do it. "You're far too emotional," they told her. "It'll freak you out."

"For some reason I really wanted to do it," says Beverly. "At first I wanted to volunteer to be a crisis intervention worker, a CIW, because I wanted to work with people on a personal level, but I wasn't trained. I thought to myself, what makes me think I could do that? I'm just a hairdresser. I wondered why some person who didn't know me would want me to visit. Now I understand how awful the isolation is for so many people, I can be a help."

In the beginning Beverly didn't tell her friends what she was doing. She didn't want people saying, "Oh my God, what if you get AIDS?" Once she did tell people, often the response was, "Do you have any cuts on you?" "You don't drink out of the glasses, do you?"

Beverly would respond casually, "Yes, I do drink out of washed glasses. You don't get AIDS that way."

Beverly did not want to put herself into a position where people wouldn't want to come near her. She likes to go out and have a good time. "Many people's reactions are frightening. One day I had a rash on my neck, and a girl at work screamed, 'Oh my goodness, do you think it's AIDS?' There's a part in me that wants to fight for the good cause, but there's another part that doesn't want to be treated badly just because I'm working with AIDS. I'm very careful about who I tell. Also, I didn't want to say, 'Look at me. I'm volunteering. Isn't that great?' I don't feel that way. Stephen, though, is so proud about my volunteering that he tells more people about it than I do."

A week after her training, Beverly was assigned to Manuel (name and identity changed). She says, "I've always been a free spirit, and I've always felt I could do whatever I want. Generally I've floated through life. Now someone was dependent upon me and I could no longer be so slapdash about things. Someone needed me and I had to be there for him even when I didn't want to be."

Manuel has Kaposi's sarcoma, an unusual form of cancer that sometimes develops when a person has AIDS. Beverly says, "The first time I met Manuel I was shocked at how sick he looked. He had no flesh on his body. He was still walking, although he was in great pain because he had nothing—no muscles—to support his bones. His body was almost dead but his spirit was strong. Before he became sick he was huge. He was a wrestler.

"I *love* Manuel. He is very stubborn. He says exactly what he thinks." When they first met, he told Beverly he only had six weeks to live. His lover, Richard (name and identity changed), with whom he lives, had ARC. Richard was not showing symptoms, so he was able to work. He kept his diagnosis a secret.

Beverly says, "In the beginning I would visit about three days a week. He didn't need someone there more often. In the morning I'd make lunch and then leave. Richard was an airline steward and had odd hours, so between us our schedule worked out well."

Manuel didn't say much at first. Eventually, he began to open up. "When I die I hope it doesn't hurt . . . I hope I will die at home." Beverly found these statements shocking and didn't know how to respond.

When Manuel was told he was close to dying, he thought he would react as they did in the movies. He said, "In the movies when a character is told he has only a month or two to live, he goes off to exotic places: Paris, China, Disneyland. I want to stay at home."

Beverly began spending her Sundays with her client. She would bring a video that they would watch together. "We'd have breakfast. Sometimes Manuel would take a nap. We got to know each other pretty well. One of the main concerns about some PWAs is that they don't go out, and their lives become empty because they just watch TV. I would take things to Manuel to keep up his interests."

Manuel loved animals. Beverly brought her dog for a visit. He enjoyed that. She brought him a book on the British royal family because he was interested in them.

Manuel adored dinosaurs. He said, "I know now that I will never see the dinosaurs in the Natural History Museum. Seeing a dinosaur before I die is such a little thing to want. It's not like dying without ever seeing Madonna."

That really upset Beverly. All the things that Manuel wanted to do were such small things. He would love to go to the movies, but he couldn't. He wanted to go to the museum, but he would never be able to.

It was very important to Beverly that she do everything Manuel wanted her to do. If he called when she was going somewhere else, she would cancel her appointment to be with him. She loaned him her TV. Team members told her she was getting in over her head, because she liked him too much. They felt she would not be able to handle it when he died. After a while Beverly questioned herself, "Are they right?"

After a great deal of thought Beverly decided she was not overly involved. "I knew that Manuel had six weeks. What can you do for a person in six weeks?"

Manuel's mother arrived from Puerto Rico. She not only had to accept the fact that her son was gay, but also that he was dying. Manuel said that his family was more upset that he was gay than that he was dying.

Beverly summed up the situation at a team meeting. "In a one bedroom apartment, Manuel is dying. His mother does not speak one word of English. She and Manuel sleep in the bedroom. Richard sleeps in the living room because he has to get up at odd hours to go to work. On top of that, the mother doesn't like Richard. I suppose she has to be angry at someone, so it might as well be Richard. Manuel's mother is nice but we can't speak to one another. We just hug each other. Manuel and his mother argue a lot because they're together all day. Richard and Manuel argue. They are all cooped up together."

"I've been thinking," Manuel said one night on the telephone with Beverly. "I've been conservative all my life. I would like to be outrageous. I would like to have a really outrageous haircut before I die." Manuel was losing some of his hair because he was on chemotherapy.

Beverly suggested that he think about the haircut some more. Then if he really wanted it, she would ask Stephen to come over and cut it for him. "I'm sure he won't mind," she told him. Beverly doesn't cut hair. She does coloring and manages Stephen's shop.

Manuel called her back and said he really wanted to have his hair done. Beverly asked Stephen if he would do a Mohawk. "We went up to the apartment the next day. Stephen was shocked by the way Manuel looked. He had never seen anyone that sick." He swallowed his fear, picked up his tools, and, though Beverly could have done it herself, he dyed Manuel's hair bright orange.

When Manuel's mother walked into the room, she shrieked in horror. Stephen looked up and smiled a how-do-ya-do as he continued working. Beverly gaily waved hello and handed Stephen an electric razor. No longer fearful, Stephen began shaving the sides of Manuel's head.

Manuel's mother thought her son had finally gone crazy. As Beverly held her in her arms, she sat there rocking from side to side and crying. And Manuel? He sat up in his bed with a beatific grin, proud as a peacock.

"That evening Manuel called to say he had not been so happy since he became sick. It meant so much to him that he could do that. It meant a lot to me as well," said Beverly.

Beverly harbors no illusions. "I'm not saving Manuel's life. I'm the one person he can call up at any time and say, 'Do something for me.' That's a big help, but at the end of the day, he's still dying. I can't change that. I'm not a therapist and I'm not going to go around telling people what to do. I decided to help in a practical way. When I look at Manuel's mother I wonder why she is not freaking out. If I came down with AIDS, I don't know how I would tell my family. I can't imagine handling death as nobly as Manuel does. He's very calm and collected. I'd be terrified."

Manuel often tells Beverly how wonderful she is and how glad he is that she can do this for him. She says he gives her more than she gives to him.

"He gives me a sense of love. It sounds stupid, but I have a very honest love for Manuel. He taught me that I am able to love someone simply because he's a human being, irrespective of anything else."

Sister Kathleen

Kathleen is a Franciscan nun. She lives according to the rule of St. Francis. When the Saint came upon a leper on the road whom everyone else shunned, Francis gave him his cloak and then embraced him. In medieval times, lepers were isolated and abandoned by society, just like many people with AIDS today. Kathleen searched for a means to reach out to PWAs as Francis did to the lepers. A priest suggested that the best way to do that was through GMHC. She looked into what the organization had to offer and decided to become a buddy.

She helped in the education office until she could take the training course. She was immediately assigned to Mark (name and identity changed).

At first Kathleen felt awkward. Although she was quite comfortable with spiritual intimacies, physical contact such as holding a person or giving a back rub was not natural for her. "Mark was a quiet person," she says. "I told him I was a nun and he looked at me as if I had four heads."

To his friends he would say, "I don't know why *she* comes to visit me."

One day when Kathleen was visiting, Mark was very depressed and started to cry. Kathleen put her arms around him, timidly. "Mark, don't

Sister Kathleen

cry. There are people who love you and care about you. You're not alone." She mentioned all his friends.

He looked up at her and said, "You're my good friend, too."

Kathleen speaks softly when she refers to people who have AIDS. "These are young people, gentle people. Beautiful young people who are dying much too soon. I've held them in my arms as they died. I've watched them as they fought to live. In my life I've never seen such bravery."

*   *   *

Beside being a buddy, Kathleen continued to volunteer in the GMHC education office. Whenever a person was needed to give lectures or make phone calls, she was there. "How could I refuse?" she says. "They are doing such wonderful work. I'll do anything for them."

Holding a condom, Sister Kathleen stood before a small group of women. She explained how it worked and showed how to put it on. In the past, only gay men came to safer sex forums, but lately, more and more women have shown up.

Kathleen told the women to insist that their partners wear a condom. She explained that a spermicide would give added protection and a water-based lubricant would prevent the condom from tearing. "That prevents it from bursting. Some of them didn't know that. Here I am, a celibate, telling sexually active women how to protect themselves. My face gets red every time I think about it."

This particular meeting was attended by young, middle-aged, and older women. They came from vastly different backgrounds, but they had one thing in common: They were all fearful. One woman was having a relationship with a man who, she recently learned, was an intravenous drug abuser. Her boyfriend might have AIDS and not know it, so she was at risk. Another woman was married to a hemophiliac. Several years ago, before all donated blood was screened, he had a blood transfusion and now he has AIDS. Having unprotected sex could give her AIDS too.

When Kathleen told Team Seven about her latest job, everyone cracked up. Kachin, astounded, asked her, "How do you, a nun, show how to put on a condom?"

"Oh, I use a banana. It's the second best model." Kathleen blushed, and the team howled with laughter.

5 · I BUMP INTO THINGS

Kachin dropped by Michael's apartment after the team meeting, and found he wasn't feeling well. He told her he became dizzy when he walked fast.

Kachin tried to alleviate his concern. "You were in the hospital so long. Recovery takes time. If I stay in bed for a week, I know I have to take it slowly."

Michael said, "I bump into things."

Kachin suggested he should mention it to the doctor.

"I told him. The doctor said he'll take care of one problem at a time."

Kachin laughed and Michael smiled sheepishly.

Michael could see that Kachin was distracted, and he asked what was wrong. She replied, "I'm thinking of taking the AIDS test. In the future I would like to have children."

Michael asked, "What if it came back positive?"

"I would give up any thoughts about having kids."

"Take someone with you when you are tested. Don't go alone," Michael said. "I went by myself. I knew I was antibody positive. Once Juan came down with it, I was sure I would get it."

Michael and Kachin silently held hands. In almost a whisper Michael said, "Why was he taken away from me? I feel so lost. So lonely, so empty, so angry. If I could only bring him back, bring him back healthy."

Michael understood that he must regain the positive attitude he had

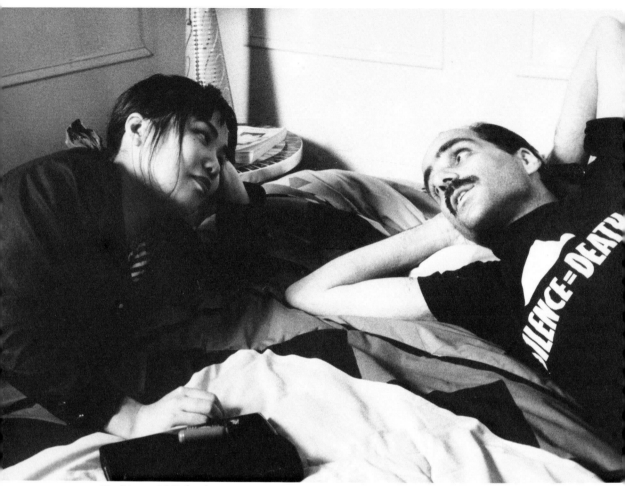

Kachin and Michael

throughout his life if he was to fight his disease. During the oddest times, though, his thoughts would turn pessimistic. He would wonder what his next infection would be, and when he would have to return to the hospital. At unexpected moments he would burst into tears. He felt like a human time bomb.

He told Kachin, "When I sleep I hear someone talking to me. It sounds so real. Then I wake up and realize that I am alone. Maybe it's Juan."

Kachin held his hand. "You're a tough guy."

"I am. I wouldn't be here if I weren't."

6 · MEETING AT CHURCH

As the director of religious education in her parish, Sister Kathleen worked with programs for people who were homeless, elderly, or homebound. She wanted to add a program to help people with AIDS. She called the education department at GMHC for advice about setting up a group of volunteer lawyers and financial advisers from her church who would work for PWAs in the community. Then there were the babies.

The Surgeon General's Workshop on Children with HIV Infection and Their Families reported, "About two-thirds of pediatric AIDS cases are the result of transmission from the infected (pregnant) mother to (her) child. . . . Most of these mothers are intravenous drug abusers or sex partners of drug abusers or of bisexual men. . . .

"There is a lack of foster care placement for HIV infected infants and children. Pediatric units are overwhelmed by the social and medical demands of both ill and well children with HIV infection. There are not enough hospital personnel to provide and coordinate multi-disciplinary inpatient, outpatient, community care, and just plain hugging and playing with these children."

With that report in mind, Kathleen decided to start a new church activity with her teen leaders' group. The kids would visit babies with AIDS in the hospitals, play with them, read stories to them, and show the babies that they were loved.

Kathleen called Tom Riley, Jr. (name and identity changed), a popular, athletic sixteen-year-old who could, she thought, influence the other kids to join the program. She often asked Tom to lead various church and community teen projects and he always came through for her. She told him her idea. Tom had heard about the babies' plight on TV and he immediately jumped at the chance to start the program.

At church the following Sunday, Kathleen saw Tom's father and told him about her plan. Tom Sr. was enthusiastic as well. It was important to him that his son help less fortunate people. Kathleen set up an appointment with the father and son to work out the details of the project the following evening.

Mr. Riley came from Ireland with his family when he was fifteen. A proud, naturalized citizen, he finished high school and joined the Marines where he served with distinction in Vietnam. Later he managed and worked in the same neighborhood restaurant for twenty years. He is the father of seven children, and after his wife died four years ago in a car accident, he has been raising the children alone.

When Mr. Riley walked into the rectory of St. Stephen's church, followed by Tom, he was upset. While he shook hands with Sister Kathleen, he was careful not to look into her eyes.

Mr. Riley spoke first. "Just as I was leaving for our meeting my boss called to ask if I could work the after-theater shift. When I explained that I was meeting you about a teen volunteer program for AIDS babies, he went crazy.

" 'AIDS? Are you nuts! You'd let your kid be around AIDS? What kind of father are you?'

"I tried to tell him that you can't get AIDS through casual contact. I tried to make him understand, to educate him. He wouldn't hear anything.

" 'If you let Tom near those babies, he's never to walk into my restaurant. Tom and everyone else in your family. I don't want to become contaminated.' He was actually screaming at me."

Mr. Riley continued, "This may be New York, but we live in a small neighborhood. Every one knows everyone else's business. When you first told me about your program, I liked it. It never occurred to me that other people would be against it."

Tom sat quietly in the corner as his father talked. Sister Kathleen knew she must remain patient. "This is why we need to educate people. They just do not understand," she said.

"People like my boss don't want to be educated. They are set in their ways. Maybe the next generation will be better. Meanwhile, what am I to do? I'm comfortable with Tom doing this kind of work, but what if our friends and neighbors turn their backs on us? What if they think of me as an irresponsible father? What if I lose my job? I have eight mouths to feed. I feel sorry for those babies, but I can't afford to lose my job over it."

"Why would you lose it?" Sister Kathleen asked.

"Sister, don't you realize how afraid people are of AIDS? Two queer-looking fellows came into the restaurant the other day and ordered hamburgers and a couple of beers. We served them. After they left, the owner took all the dishes and threw them into the garbage. He sees a gay person and sees AIDS right away. That owner won't let Tom into his bar or even let me serve drinks if my son works with children with AIDS."

Kathleen was astonished. She had forgotten that many people still harbored prejudices about AIDS.

"Do you mean that if I, *Sister* Kathleen, had dinner at your bar you would throw out *my* dishes?"

"Well, not yours, of course . . ."

"Why not? Every day I work with people who have AIDS."

"But that's different."

"How is it different?" She pressed him.

"What can I say?"

Kathleen changed her approach. She said that this was a Franciscan church dedicated to the rule of St. Francis. She talked about how Francis gave his cloak to a cold and exhausted leper whom everyone else shunned. Instead of catching leprosy, he found God. Before that he was a playboy—a generous playboy. She told how he used to hang out in the bars and treat everybody to drinks.

Knowing she had their attention, she said, "The lepers were isolated and completely abandoned by society, just like the person with AIDS is today. Kaposi's sarcoma causes lesions all over the body. It isn't too pretty and neither is leprosy. And babies with AIDS are surely today's forgotten people. We must reach out to them as Francis did to the lepers."

Mr. Riley listened quietly. "How do you feel about it, Tom?" he asked his son.

"I want to do it. You know I want to help, and I could get a bunch of other kids to help, too. I'm not worried about getting AIDS. We learned all about that in school. If anyone tries to mess with me about it, I can handle it. I don't care what the bigots think." He looked toward Kathleen. "But I'm worried about my father. He has to live with these people, work with them. If he lost his job because of my volunteer work, what would happen to our family?"

Mr. Riley said, "When I was a boy in Ireland, I did volunteer work. I worked in an old folks' home for people with incurable illnesses. It was very rewarding. That was different. Everyone praised me for what I did."

"People would praise Tom in the same way," said Sister Kathleen quickly. After more discussion, everyone became quiet.

Sister Kathleen broke the silence, "You need time to think this through. I've been so closely involved with AIDS that I've forgotten how frightening it is to people who aren't educated about it. Take some time, Tom, talk to your friends. Maybe they'll surprise you. Then decide."

Sister Kathleen called Tom the next day, to let him off the hook. "I'm not going to proceed with the babies' project," she said. "I'm not ready. I'll put it on hold."

7 · MIKE FRASCH, TEAM NURSE

Mike Frasch, Team Seven's nurse, spends his day ministering to the needs of the patients on his floor at Cabrini Medical Center. This week over a hundred people were undergoing treatment for AIDS related illnesses, and Mike, who considered himself high risk, empathized with each of them.

He says, "By the seventh grade, I knew that I was gay. I come from a little town upstate. At that time they didn't know what the word *gay* meant. Everybody called gays 'queer.' When I reached eighteen, I couldn't handle being gay in a small town."

The Vietnam war was going on and Mike didn't want to go into the service.

Mike thought of becoming a nurse, but he saw that this choice would put him on his own, facing his problems with homosexuality and the draft. His family was ardently Catholic and Mike had gone to Catholic schools. He decided to join the seminary. There everything was taken care of, and in many ways it was an easy life. Mike became a Jesuit and taught high-school English.

"There was more to it," he says. "Something inside me made me enter the order. I always had a strong faith, a belief in God. I wanted to be of service. My parents were thrilled."

Once in the seminary, Mike lived a frustrated life. He had no sex because he took his vows very seriously. When he knew he could no longer

Mike, Dr. Montana and Walter (PWA)

stand being celibate, he left. Mike anguished and prayed over his decision. He had been a Jesuit ten years. "It was not that I left because I didn't believe the Gospels any more or because I was angry with religion. I left because I reached a point where I wasn't going to live the vows."

Mike went back to school and became a nurse. It was scary at thirty to be out on his own for the first time. Getting an apartment, paying rent, finding a job was new to him. But he did it.

In 1981, people began coming to the emergency room of his hospital with a strange illness. The disease didn't even have a name then. The fear of an unknown disease hitting one particular group was incredible. Patients were put into isolation. Everyone wore masks and gowns when treating them.

As Mike saw the numbers of gay people diagnosed with this nameless disease increasing, and the same patients returning to the emergency room again and again, he thought, my God, this could be me.

Mike tries to maintain a positive attitude with patients, but sometimes it is difficult. "I try to make the patients feel hopeful. I tell them to give the medications a chance, and not to give up. If they ask me if they are going to die, I won't lie to them. I tell them they probably will. I also say that it is the quality of the life that they have left that counts now. They have the power to make a lot of changes, and there is time to put things together."

AIDS has changed Mike's life drastically. Things that he would normally take for granted have become very special. Before, he would get up in the morning and complain because he had to go to work. At the hospital now he might take forty-five minutes to help a twenty-year-old AIDS patient to the bathroom. "How can I possibly complain about getting up for work?"

At first Mike spent much of his free time visiting people with AIDS. He followed up on fifty patients outside the hospital. "I would work eight hours with AIDS patients and then visit others at home. I befriended many people only to watch them die. Nights I went to bed crying. I had horrible dreams. For a while, I went to the funerals and the wakes of all my patients. But it got to be too much, and I realized that wasn't a healthy way to function."

Mike learned about GMHC from the buddies who visited the patients. He went to the GMHC office and signed up.

Because he worked directly with patients at the hospital, he never took a client of his own. He volunteered as the team nurse for four different buddy teams. No one on a team can ask Mike specific information about a patient because that is confidential. But if someone says the client has PCP, Mike explains what symptoms to look out for once the client is sent home.

Mike gets many phone calls from the buddies, even in the middle of the night. They describe what symptoms their clients are experiencing and ask what they should do. He doesn't mind the calls at all. He feels that he's doing more for God now than he did during his seminary years.

Mike said that when he left the seminary and was free from his vows he was "sleazy" for two years. He was going to make up for lost time. After a year and a half, AIDS hit. When all this came out he thought, my God, back to celibacy. Perhaps he should have stayed in the seminary.

Recently Mike found that he had been going to work and buddy meetings exhausted. He was working double shifts, and a number of favorite patients had recently died. But there was more. He wondered why he was so tired, and why he was running fevers. Should he be tested? No. He couldn't handle that. He was afraid that if he tested positive, the hospital might push him out. He felt he could not give up his work.

Deep down Mike was convinced that he was HIV positive. Maybe that was why he was so comfortable with the AIDS patients. "When I saw them, I saw me."

Mike

Mike called Michael for advice. Through Kathleen and Kachin, they had become friends. Michael encouraged Mike to take the HIV blood test, because he felt that Mike could handle the results.

Mike called the AIDS hotline in Brooklyn. They asked him to make up a three-digit code to ensure confidentiality. They immediately began asking specific sexual questions that shocked Mike. There he was in the hallway of his hospital answering these questions, and wondering if someone would walk by and hear him. An appointment for the test was made for the following month.

When the day arrived, many friends offered to go with him, but Mike chose to do it alone. It seemed like any other day. He found the last seat on the Second Avenue downtown bus. He carried copies of *The New York Times, The Daily News,* and a small assortment of GMHC education leaflets that he purposely left on the empty seats of the bus, thinking that someone might pick one up and learn something.

At the Department of Health, he gave the receptionist his secret code number, and was handed a consent form that listed the risks of the tests.

First, Mike met with a psychologist, a huge "mother earth" type who had four children. She asked more intimate questions and talked about the testing process. Mike thought she was the perfect person to be a counselor because she made him feel totally at ease. Drawing blood for the test was no different from the procedure he had performed himself thousands of times.

Mike had to wait three weeks for the results of the test. He threw himself into his work. Michael and other friends and buddies called him several times a week to see how he was doing. Mike tried to play it down. As far as he was concerned, he said to them, he was positive and this test would confirm it. No one at the hospital where he worked was told.

When the results were still a week away, Mike realized his apartment was about to be painted. He rationalized that he should not cope with the chaos in his home at the same time as a positive test, and he called the Department of Health to postpone his appointment. The psychologist who made him feel so comfortable answered his call and said, "The results are in. Can you come in today?"

Then Mike was *sure* it was positive. He says, "I went nuts."

First, he had to finish his shift. The nurse who was to relieve him was late. "I was flying around being busy. I was in and out of my patients' rooms. Still, I couldn't help worrying that I would be late. I got into a taxi and I don't remember getting out. Once inside the health department, I gave my number to the receptionist. The way the receptionist looked at me, I was sure she knew. I had carefully rehearsed what I was going to say to the psychologist. I'd start with, 'I guess it's positive.'"

Mike walked into the office. He said, "Well, I guess it's . . ." The psychologist interrupted, "Before you get upset, it came back negative." Mike was speechless.

"Aren't you excited?" she asked. Mike couldn't believe the results. She admitted that she was surprised, too, considering Mike's sexual history, and she suggested that he redo the test, just to confirm the diagnosis.

Right after the appointment, Mike stopped over at Michael's apartment to return some books and tell him the test results. Michael was very excited for him.

That night Mike called all his friends who had been so supportive. Nearly everyone was thrilled, but there were a few surprises. Mike could tell by their voices that some friends who were diagnosed positive were not enthusiastic. Did they feel abandoned?

One person, who had insisted that Mike take the test, lashed out in anger. Mike didn't know what to say. It put an end to the friendship.

But Michael was just the opposite. He was always supportive. Mike says, "Here was a person, himself diagnosed with AIDS, truly encouraging me. As buddies, *we're* supposed to encourage *them*. It's wonderful when it turns around and the person with AIDS supports us. I really get a lot from Michael."

Two weeks later, the second report came in negative. The psychologist was delighted. She gave Mike a big hug and kiss.

Mike says the test result has changed him. He says, "I'm much calmer. I can take myself out of their picture when I work. My interest in AIDS hasn't changed. I used to think, that's me. Now I look at these young kids and think, why should it be them?"

8 · BUDDY MEETING

Sister Kathleen rushed up the steps to Brooke's apartment eager to share her latest GMHC assignment with Team Seven. Her safe sex lectures were becoming so successful that the education department had asked her to talk on Cable TV. Some team members asked if it was for a gay TV station. "No," Kathleen explained, her face turning beet red, "they use the porno station." The team members loved it. When Kathleen told her Monsignor about the upcoming lecture, he asked, "With or without your clothes?"

"Why me?" she sighed.

The meeting came to order after all those present were seated, drinks in hand. Warren began by welcoming David Smith's return to the team. David had taken time off from the team when he himself was diagnosed with AIDS. Now feeling healthy, he was eager to assist the group and act as a back-up for his teammates' clients.

Another welcome was for the surprise visit by John Campanella, one of GMHC's original team captains. Lately, John had been visiting teams captained by members of his initial team. John had trained Warren.

John's meetings had been orderly and formal, and he ran a tight ship. Warren and Brooke's were very different. Team Seven joked, yelled, argued. Everybody laughed. They disagreed philosophically over many issues, which wasn't surprising, given their different backgrounds.

A Team Seven meeting

The buddies began their reports. Kachin reported that Michael was still in mourning for Juan. He would begin to take the drug, AZT, as part of his treatment. John Campanella advised that everyone reacts to the drug differently. Both Michael and Kachin were well aware that there can be dangerous side effects, but Michael was optimistic about the forthcoming treatment. David Smith gave Kachin a copy of the latest findings from the original study on AZT. Like David, Michael would probably take two blue and white capsules every four hours, every day, for the rest of his life.

Then it was Beverly's turn. When Beverly first met her client, Manuel, he had been given six weeks to live. That was seven months ago and even though he could barely move, he still held tight to his powerful will to survive. Beverly told the team how ironic it was that Manuel's lover, Richard, who had been working, feeling fine, and had concealed the fact that he had ARC from his co-workers, had recently been hospitalized with AIDS.

Manuel was also in the hospital and down to 102 pounds. His stay was all the more painful because he was unable to help Richard, who was at another hospital. Beverly spent a lot of time with Manuel because the only other person to visit him was his mother. It worried Beverly that Manuel was in so much pain. John Campanella asked if he was on a particular type of chemotherapy. Beverly was amazed how John zeroed in on the cause of Manuel's suffering.

John, who confronts tough issues head on, spoke easily from first-hand experience, because he too has AIDS. He said, "Because PWAs all share the latest information, they are often ahead of the doctors—which can be unnerving for both of us. Sometimes I tell my doctors things that I would want *him* to tell *me*. When I became a PWA, I picked up as much information as I could because it was *my* life that was threatened."

Joe Dolce arrived late. He was shaking. A very close friend of his had just been diagnosed. Warren had a client in need of a buddy, and he asked Joe to take him on. Joe, still devastated by Anthony's death, declined. He didn't feel ready for another client, and he was considering leaving the team in order to form a writing group for the GMHC recreation center.

James Baggett also had a close friend in the hospital. "When I saw my friend, I felt as if he was looking deep into my soul. His eyes were a curious combination of peaceful resolution and glassy horror." Some people describe this gaze as the hopeless look that can be seen in the eyes of the starving in Ethiopia and India. When a person is very ill with AIDS, that same look often appears. Once he is well again, the look is gone. James found his friend's eyes frightening.

Brooke, who had taken a new client to relieve the growing backlog of PWAs waiting for buddies, gave her report. Though she thought her client was very sweet, she was distressed that he would not do anything for himself. Trying to second guess what he needed was difficult. He would never ask for anything; rather, he would hint that he might want something. "I don't know what to do. Should I be more aggressive?" she asked the team. Ed Hartmann, the most experienced member of the team, suggested a support group. The client had told Brooke that he wanted to go into therapy but he never followed up on it.

Once, when Brooke was at a rehearsal, Beverly called Brooke's client to be sure he had enough food in his apartment. He told her he didn't know. "If he doesn't know, how do *I* know?" said Beverly throwing up her hands in frustration.

Brooke once asked him, "Are you going to have dinner?"

"Yeah, I guess so," he replied uninterested.

"What are you going to have?"

"I don't know. I still have some chicken breast there from last week."

Trying to be practical, Brooke bought him a number of frozen dinners so that he would always have well-balanced food at hand in case of an emergency.

Beverly had also helped Brooke clean his filthy apartment. That was three weeks ago, the last time it was cleaned. Beverly griped that he did nothing to be independent.

Dave Smith said, "You can't expect him to be cheerful and say 'Whoopee, we're having veal tonight.'" David said it was easier for a PWA to just let life wind down. "As I listen to this dinner conversation I realize that I, having AIDS, am often in that same predicament. I will sit in my kitchen and think, do I really give a damn what I eat? There are larger questions I must deal with now. Old priorities, such as what do I want to eat, no longer seem important."

Brooke understood David's attitude, but she was still distressed that she was unable to make her client's day-to-day existence easier. How could the buddies perform best?

"If you want to clean his apartment, do it," David recommended. "If the dirt piles up, that doesn't matter either. Sometimes that's the way one deals with being ill."

Dave Fisher remarked that his client, an artist, had stopped painting. Dave had naively asked him, "Why don't you paint?" He told Dave that he didn't feel like it anymore. "So what am I supposed to say to that? That's his privilege."

The team meeting was drawing to a close. Many gathered around John Campanella as he talked comfortably about his diagnosis. David Smith touched Beverly's shoulder. "If you need a back-up with Manuel, I will be glad to help out."

"Thanks," said Beverly, "I appreciate that."

Warren looked at the pile of buddy reports in front of him. He was perplexed. "GMHC has thirty clients awaiting buddies," he said to no one in particular.

James Baggett overheard. "I can handle another client."

Dave Fisher, the most soft-spoken member, said, "Me, too."

Joe Dolce, leaving the apartment, turned around. Leaning heavily against the door he raised his index finger. "Count me in."

John Campanella

In early 1983, when AIDS was becoming an epidemic, John joined the Gay Men's Health Crisis. He volunteered to work with AIDS because he is homosexual. He understood, however, that he might be taking care of a woman, a drug abuser, anyone. That didn't matter to him because he saw this epidemic as one that not only affected his community but the entire world, which is also his community.

When GMHC began to form the buddies into neighborhood teams, John became a team captain. At the same time he was the manager of the volunteer office.

Running the volunteer office meant dealing with many different personalities. It was literally group therapy from seven in the morning till midnight. Weekends were the only time he could go to the office alone, think, make evaluations. GMHC consumed him. His life had become loveless, sexless, even movieless. During this time, he and his lover, on shaky grounds anyway, broke up.

John recalls the executive director of GMHC telling him, "When the day comes that you leave the volunteer office, your one consolation will be that you will never again have to work as hard." And that was true.

Eventually John stopped being a buddy captain because he became absolutely exhausted. Although he was making his calls to the buddies and their clients, and he was holding meetings, his heart wasn't in it anymore.

John

He resigned all his posts at GMHC. "My goal was to forget about AIDS for a while. I needed a personal life. I hated GMHC. I hated Kaposi's sarcoma. I hated anything that came near this disease. Of course, my fear was that I'd be diagnosed and be back in it all over again."

Two weeks later, John was in New York hospital with pneumocystis carinii pneumonia (PCP). He had AIDS.

For the first three days after his diagnosis, John refused to talk with anyone who had AIDS, because, like many people, he was denying that he had the disease. By not telling anybody about it, he thought he could control his diagnosis.

John remained in the hospital for eleven days. The three months after he was discharged were the hardest. "I was learning a new career. I was consumed with pills and bills and reading—a colossal amount of reading—and doctor appointments and psychological considerations for myself and for the people around me."

John's role models, once he got his diagnosis, were the other men and women he knew who had AIDS. When he left the hospital, he touched base with all the clients he knew who were surviving. He wanted to see if they had anything in common. Was there a silver thread woven through this? He learned that the common thread was that each survivor had a powerful belief in something. Jesus. Macrobiotic food. Yoga. Whatever it was, they believed strongly and that kept them going.

"People who were resigned to the fact that they had a fatal illness usually died pretty quickly. The people who were fighters seemed to be around longer. I had something, a keen love for wildlife, which has been the source of my greatest happiness."

Much against his doctor's recommendation, John planned to take his vacation seeing wildlife in the national preserve in Nepal. "You don't go to microorganism land when you have a suppressed immune system," the doctor warned him.

John replied, "I'm not going to be any more afraid to live than I am to die."

He went to Nepal and for a while he was able to forget that he had AIDS. The only time he thought about it was when he spent two days in India on his way home. "From New Delhi I went to visit the Taj Mahal with the masses, and I mean the masses. It was frightening. No one spoke English. I was entirely alone. Even buying my ticket and getting on the right train was a challenge. The temperature was 116. There was fecal matter and urine everywhere. A man was brushing his teeth in the water fountain next to me. Women and men carrying bundles and babies pushed and shoved. That's when I said, 'Gee, I have a suppressed immune system.'"

The train ride to the Taj Mahal lasted three hours and John sat in a small cubicle with eight other people. Some of them were sleeping or eating in the luggage racks above him. They kept dropping things on him. He was frightened.

John's refrigerator

"When I saw the Taj Mahal, a year after I had been diagnosed, I had tears in my eyes. I felt very grateful."

One result of John's diagnosis was that he felt he had been totally inadequate in his previous role as a buddy and crisis intervention worker. Only now did he know what the disease was all about. He joined GMHC again as a volunteer, something he had sworn he would never do. Under the circumstances he wanted to help somebody who might be a lot sicker than he was, and who perhaps knew a great deal less than he did.

"My first client was a newly diagnosed twenty-three-year-old fellow who lived in my neighborhood. He was terror-stricken. He was so paranoid that he would not go outside because he thought people would know that he had AIDS. I asked him if I looked like I had AIDS. He said no and I told him, 'Well, I do.' That's all he had to hear. He needed a role model. And I needed to do that for somebody."

John says that he doesn't have the anger about dying that the younger guys experience. "They feel as if they have to leave in the middle of the movie. There's been much richness in my life. I've had a lot of love and a lot of friends. I've traveled a great deal. I don't feel cheated. In some ways, strange as it seems, I don't regret having AIDS. It has been such a challenge and such a battle. I've gotten to know myself even better because of it. I've learned how to deal with a crisis and I know what my resources are. I've come to appreciate myself more and love myself more. That doesn't mean I wouldn't like another forty-four years."

John grew up as a Roman Catholic. He believed that when you die, you went to heaven, hell, or purgatory. You atoned for your sins, and went to heaven. Over the years he got away from that. He became a humanist, believing that the spirit is always there. "I thought that you died and came back as a snail or a tree or another human being."

John eventually came to believe there is no life after death. After his diagnosis he asked his very diverse crowd of friends what they thought about death. He was amazed at how many felt as he did.

"If I could say, no matter how much I suffer or how early I die, there is this other world I'm going to, new horizons, a new life, that would make it a lot easier. It's much more difficult when you believe as I do."

9 · DENNIS

Joe Dolce put on a black-and-white checked shirt, matching hat, and black baggy pants. Before leaving his apartment he called his new client to be sure everything was okay. His client was feeling fine. Joe checked his watch. He had fifteen minutes to bicycle to his first creative writing class at the GMHC recreation center. It began to thunder, and he wondered whether anyone would show up. By the time he arrived, it was pouring. Joe was convinced no one would go out on such a miserable night.

At a large round table a solitary young man sat waiting for the writer's class to begin. This was Dennis. Joe and he chatted cordially while waiting for others to arrive. "I'm not sure I'm a writer," he told Joe in a subdued voice, "but I have a story inside me that must get out." Joe listened with absolute concentration. He was staggered by what Dennis told him.

Dennis's story:

"I was a skinny kid who people made fun of. To counter their teasing, I did dangerous things. I wasn't out for a laugh, I was out for a *WOW*. I would do anything to get attention. And I mean anything. When stories were told that people died swimming in the East River, I was the one to jump into it.

"I grew up in a house where alcoholism ran rampant. Several of my relatives were alcoholics. Our house was the meeting-place for their parties. There was a room next to my brothers' and my bedroom that my mother kept for drying out. My brothers and I called it the 'rubber room' because that's what they call the padded rooms for crazy people in the nut houses.

"As a little kid I would lie in bed, scared, because all I heard from the 'rubber room' were the screams and horrors of one of my relatives trying to kick alcohol.

"When I became a teenager, the last place where I wanted to be was in that house. It had only bad memories for me, real bad memories.

"In the sixties, when I was entering high school, there were two crowds: the hippies and the juice heads. The juice heads were the jocks who drank. The hippies were the political demonstrators who smoked pot.

Dennis and Joe

"During those years the choice was booze or pot. Between the ages of thirteen and fifteen, my crowd graduated very quickly from marijuana to amphetamines to sniffing glue.

"Besides heroin and methadone, I have an addiction to sniffing glue. I'm amazed that I can even put a sentence together today when I read how many brain cells are killed from sniffing glue.

"When I first sniffed glue, it gave me a feeling of being out of this world and into another where everything looked and sounded different. My body vibrated. I would do anything that would take me out of myself.

"Drugs were becoming very heavy in high school. I was doing marijuana and 'ups.' I tripped on acid hundreds of times. I was so into acid that at one point I tried to shoot it. In fact you can't shoot LSD—but I tried."

The park where Dennis hung out had two sections: one was called "Pill Hill" and the other "Dope Slope." His crowd stayed on Dope Slope.

Then heroin came to the neighborhood. "I had no reservations about snorting heroin. I was the first one on my block to do it. The first time I did it, I was in love. I knew that I had found what I was looking for. I had tried every single drug available and none of them came close to what heroin did for me. It made me feel it no longer mattered if I was accepted. I didn't have to be a phony. It was okay for me to be alone, nodding out somewhere. I started neglecting my girlfriend. I would say that I loved heroin more than I loved her, and I loved her very much."

Dennis snorted heroin for a year and a half. His friends swore they would never shoot heroin, only snort it, but Dennis never said that.

He began to go where all the junkies, older, tough guys, stayed. One was an old-time junkie called P.K. Dennis went to the abandoned building where he lived and told P.K. he wanted to learn to shoot up.

"He didn't try to talk me out of it. He said, 'Come on.'

"I was scared. I put my arm out and he hit me. He put the thing in my vein and all of a sudden, I was in heaven. I now *knew* that this was the only way. He taught me how to do it. The high lasted all day long, in the beginning. When it wore off, I wasn't sick, and I wasn't depressed. But it didn't take long for me to want more because I loved it. By five o'clock every afternoon, I was already thinking about where I could get four or five dollars to buy more. I conned my mother. 'I'm looking for a job, Ma, I need carfare.' When I was a senior in high school, my teachers thought I had so much potential that they invited me to student-teach freshman Spanish. They also knew I was doing heavy drugs."

Dennis's teachers became very concerned about him because they saw what was happening. Often he went to school wasted. He would shoot up in the school bathrooms. The vice principal figured out what he was doing and tried hard to catch him, but he couldn't. He raided Dennis's locker once and didn't find a thing. Dennis kept the dope on his person because he knew they couldn't search him. One day the vice principal confronted Dennis in the hall. He said, "I've got to catch you. If I don't, the drugs will catch you later."

Dennis was twenty years old the first time he OD'd. The police found him at two in the morning in the middle of Northern Boulevard in Queens. It was winter. Dennis says, "I had no socks. No shoes. No coat. No nothing. I don't know how I got there. I was lying in the middle of the highway, freezing."

The police drove him to Elmhurst Hospital. He says, "I had hypothermia and I was in overdose. All I can remember is being with some guy, shooting dope in a basement."

Doctors and therapists pressed Dennis's parents to be hard on their son. They said that the only way Dennis would go straight was for his parents to kick him out of the house. When he finally got sick enough, he'd go for help. But Dennis's mother couldn't do that. She thought he would die out on the streets.

Dennis got a job with the telephone company, but that didn't last long. He was engaged to a young woman whom he had been seeing since he was seventeen, but that wouldn't last much longer, either. Dennis promised his family that he would try to break his habit, and he agreed to go on methadone in order to be weaned off heroin.

At a clinic, methadone was substituted for Dennis's heroin habit as a way to ease him off drugs. Dennis abused the methadone. He took extra from the black market, and there was a liquor store on the corner, so he had everything he needed.

Someone told Dennis that if he took Valium with the methadone, the heroin high would return. He tried it, but it didn't last, so he started shooting cocaine. Dennis became a worse abuser on methadone than when he was only shooting heroin.

One day Dennis was outside the methadone program building, feeling depressed and afraid that his impending wedding might not come off. He took two doses of methadone and fifteen doses of 10 mg. Valium. Then he popped two Elavil, an antidepressant drug given to mentally disturbed people to keep them tranquilized, and downed it all with a pint of Thunderbird.

While walking down the street, he began to feel the first effects of the pills, the liquor, and drugs. He was sure he was going to die. He started panicking, and without looking, he ran out onto Queens Boulevard, where he was hit by a cab. Police rushed him to the hospital.

Dennis went into cardiac arrest. A defibrillator, a machine used to give the heart a strong electric shock, pounded his chest to keep his heart going. He was in a coma for eleven days.

When he finally opened his eyes, his entire family was around the bed. The doctor was there, too. The doctor smiled at Dennis and said, "Dennis, that was close. We almost lost you."

Dennis looked up at him. "You miserable son-of- . . ."

"Dennis, what's the matter with you?" his sister shouted, embarrassed. "You almost died."

"That's the whole idea," he told her. "I can't take it no more."

Dennis's family promised to get him help. They put him into a detox program where he could kick his habit.

Dennis became obsessed about his fiancée. He thought she didn't know where he was, but she knew. Not long after Dennis arrived at the hospital, he was asked into the director's office. He sat down and was offered a cigarette. The director said, "Dennis, I have to tell you this because you're going to have to cope with it sooner or later. Your fiancée has left you. She asked me to tell you that she loves you very much. She loves you so much that she can't stand to see you kill yourself."

Dennis says, "I went nuts. Because I was drug free, my feelings were very raw. I cried my eyes out . . . Again . . . Again . . . Another rejection . . . Here was my chance . . . I promised to come out of the hospital and really try. But it was no good. I never, ever saw her again."

As soon as Dennis left detox, he was back on drugs. He was angry at his fiancée so he had a reason to be high.

Then suddenly Dennis decided he didn't want to do dope anymore. By now, thirteen friends were dead because of drugs. The price of heroin was going up from two dollars a packet to five. Dennis blamed his neighborhood for his habit. His family moved to a new neighborhood that took him away from Pill Hill and Dope Slope, and Dennis decided this was a perfect chance to change. But as soon as he put down hard drugs, he immediately turned to alcohol. He drank like a madman. He was twenty-two years old.

In spite of his drinking, Dennis began to rebuild his body. He was feeling good. He thought that once the drugs were out of his system, he would be fine. But he wasn't working on his head. He didn't realize that you can take away the drugs and still have the addict.

Although Dennis remained straight for one year, he still had the attitudes of an addict. He was defensive, he lied a lot and he was a sneak. He used women. He wanted people to feel sorry for him because of what he had been through.

By now, Dennis was unemployable and he was on welfare. "I was drinking and smoking pot every day. For me, that was clean. I was doing the best I ever did. I felt physically good, but from 1973 to 1975, I was lonely, very lonely.

"There is something in addiction called progression. When you first start shooting dope, you have to build up a tolerance and a habit. It can take weeks, it can take months. But when a person like me, who has been addicted for so many years, resumes using drugs by shooting it only once, he's had it. That's true of alcoholics too. They say, 'One drink is too many and a thousand is never enough.'"

One day when he was "clean," Dennis was playing ball in a park when a high-school friend from the old neighborhood passed by in his car. Dennis was high from drinking and smoking pot. The friend asked where he had been and invited him into the car to talk.

Dennis jumped in. His pal was on his way to shoot dope. It had been a year since Dennis had done any. He didn't bat an eyelash when he shot heroin once again. Immediately, it had him.

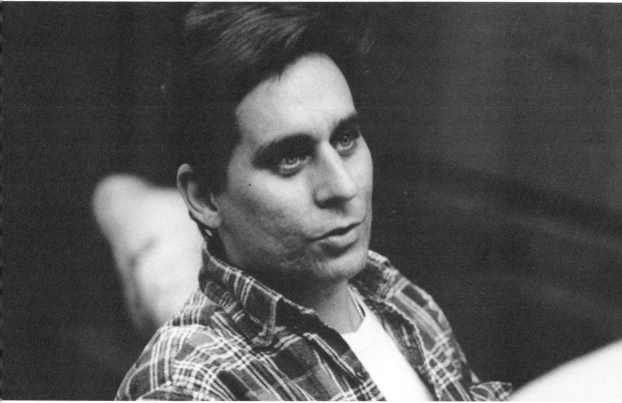

Dennis

In an abandoned building, lit by candles, twenty to thirty people would stand in puddles of dirty water sharing a needle. "I put some stranger's needle in my arm. I felt the warmth of the drug ooze into my body. When I pulled the needle out, my blood would be dripping all over the place. I'd take my hand, that was filthy from being in the abandoned building, and wipe off the blood. I was a disgusting addict."

Dennis often found it hard to get new needles. There were times when he only had enough money to buy the drug. He went to a shooting gallery where the needles were supplied.

After AIDS came into the picture, Dennis became more careful about sharing needles. He had one partner, his best friend, with whom he shared a set. Once the publicity about AIDS increased, Dennis bought his own set and saved it. He would not let anybody else use the needles and tried to keep them clean. That lasted only a little while. The point of the needle broke and the syringe became stuck. Dennis began sharing again.

By this time, Dennis had been through twenty-five hospitalizations for drug abuse. His body was in terrible shape from the dope and the many detoxes. At one hospital he was given the HIV test. It was positive. Dennis had ARC. The doctor pulled no punches, "You will die if you do not stay clean. You could be okay if you eat well, get a lot of rest, stay away from stress."

For a few days, Dennis kept his diagnosis from his family. "Then I needed to get it off my chest. I sat my mother down and said, 'Mom, listen, when I was in the hospital, I took a test for AIDS. It was positive and I've come down with ARC.'

"She just looked at me. Total fear filled her face. Finally, she cried out, 'What does that mean? Do you have it?' I tried to explain, but my mother cut in, 'Is it all right for us to come near you? Can we live in the same house? Share the same utensils? Can I touch you?' She was hysterical. Her anguish killed me. This woman, my mother, had been through hell and back with me for years, and now, this. She became so frantic, I called my doctor. She asked him millions of questions and he answered every one of them. That put her at ease a little.

"Despite all the reassurances, my mother set my own plate aside for me, my own spoon and fork. She will hug me but she won't kiss me. She will let me hug her but she doesn't want my lips to touch anybody. I feel like a leper."

Dennis brought his mother a newspaper article that pointed out that it is safe to kiss. She read it carefully, and said, "See what it says here? There is a *possibility* of catching it."

"Ma, you're looking for things."

Dennis's youngest brother is married and has a two-year-old son. When the baby comes to the house, he runs to Dennis, calling "Uncle Dennis, Uncle Dennis."

Dennis says, "I want to hug him and kiss him and I can't do it. My mother won't let me. I cried my eyes out about it. 'Please Dennis,' she begs me. 'This is our little sweetheart.'

"But Ma, I love the baby, too."

Dennis says, "I promised my parents to stop using dope. Promises, promises. Instead, my habit was getting bigger. To feed it, I stole my parents' TV. I just took it. Afterwards, I felt so guilty, I cried."

The next day, Dennis's father worried that he was going to steal the whole house so he stayed home from work. Dennis went to him for help, crying. All the detox hospitals in New York City were full. He had called Narcotics Anonymous and was told to come in the following day and stay in their office for two or three days while they got him in somewhere.

Dennis's father said, "But that's tomorrow. What are you going to do about today? You can't stay here."

"Then my 'dope-fiend' mind started working. I told my father I knew a guy who would get me a bottle of methadone for thirty dollars."

"This is against my better judgment," his father said. "I'm a recovering person myself. I know this is wrong, but I can't stand seeing you sick. Plus you got the ARC. I don't know what to do." His father was crying, too.

"My father went to the bank, cashed a check for thirty dollars, and gave it to me. I called my partner and we copped heroin."

The heroin wasn't very potent. Dennis needed more. He went home to find his father downstairs doing the laundry. "Are you okay now?" he called up to his son.

"Yes," Dennis lied. Right under the empty television table was the VCR. He took it.

Dennis stayed at the Narcotics Anonymous headquarters for three days. He had to fend for himself. He called his parents and told them he was on the Bowery. His mother was crying. "Dennis, this is our home. You've taken everything. We know you're sick. We know you have this goddamn ARC and it's killing us. We love you. We don't know what to do."

Forty-five minutes after Dennis was released from this, his twenty-sixth hospital, he found himself in his partner's car with a used needle in his arm. His partner looked at him and said, "Dennis, I hate to see you doing this to yourself." He, of course, was doing the same thing.

Dennis looked back at him. "I love you. I hate to see you doing this. It kills me." They sat there for the longest time, needles hanging from their arms, hugging each other, and crying.

Dennis remembers walking home, high from the shot. It was getting cold. The trees were becoming bare. The winter brought back memories of standing on street corners on the Lower East Side, at six in the morning, waiting to cop dope. He felt more comfortable in an abandoned building with the rats running around and a bunch of sleazy people than with his own family. He thought to himself, are you going to be out there again?

Dennis called a nurse whom he met the last time he was in detox. He told her that he had had a nervous breakdown in detox and had been put in a psych ward. Could she get him on methadone? He did not want to go through another twenty-one-day detox program.

She told him to come to the hospital to be examined by a doctor. Once there, Dennis was told, "Never mind ARC and the narcotics, you're going to die of liver disease. Your body cannot stand going through detox, getting healthy, getting sick. You need long term stabilization."

For the first time he said, *"I'll do anything that you say."* This is when he knew he was on his way to recovery. "Before this moment, I never totally surrendered. I finally had to admit that the dope kicked my ass. Once I accepted that, I could look for help. This is the only disease where once you surrender, you win.

"I told them I didn't want the pain of being addicted anymore. I would stand on my head for three days if the doctor wanted me to. I had had it. I don't want to die. I felt a load come off my back." The doctor put him on methadone again.

The methadone treatment gave him a very hard time at first, but he stuck to the prescribed doses. He went to Narcotics Anonymous and Alcoholics Anonymous. At the suggestion of his doctor, he went to Gay Men's Health Crisis where he learned more about ARC and how to live with it. He joined Joe Dolce's GMHC writing group and began writing in graphic detail about the life of an addict. Joe and the other writers in the group were impressed with his innate writing skills and encouraged him to do more.

Dennis was building a support system. Every morning at nine, he began his day at an NA meeting, and that put him in a positive frame of mind. But the old feelings, the compulsions, were still there, and he desperately wanted to stick a needle into his arm. He wanted to call his partner. But he didn't.

Dennis's parents now live in a small, three-room apartment. He sleeps on the couch. He says, "I'm grateful. It's very important for my recovery to be grateful. As an addict, I always complained about what I didn't have. I said I got a raw deal. Everything was negative. Now, I thank God that I can wake up in the morning and not have to run out and get dope. It's a blessing not to go through that insanity.

"Before, people tried to say to me, 'Dennis, you've had enough, it's time to stop.' It didn't mean a thing. When the pain became too great for me, I stopped. You have to reach your own bottom. You have to say to yourself, 'I've had it.'"

Although his doctor has given Dennis a good report about ARC, the fear of full-blown AIDS is still there. He keeps thinking that his ending is going to be a tragedy instead of a victory.

A little voice talks to him and asks, "Why are you even bothering? You're going to die." Even his therapist asked what he would do if he came down with AIDS. "No matter what, I won't return to drugs. If my ARC ever becomes AIDS, I want to die clean. I don't want to die with guilt about what I've done to my parents. Let me die knowing I've done my best. I've made peace with my parents. They understand that everything I did was not because I'm a bad person, but because I'm a sick person."

10 · SO MANY THINGS TO DO

Kachin arrived at Michael's apartment with the groceries. She hugged him and said, "You always make good lists. You are so organized. It makes my job easy."

Michael was in an up mood. He had begun taking AZT and so far, there were no side effects. He switched the subject to decorating. "I want to redo things. I want to put speakers over there. I want new bookshelves. It's a change, do you know what I mean? Change is important. I start back with my shrink on Monday. I wish I could go five times a week. I want to go to a support group at the hospital. I'm feeling stronger."

Michael helped unpack the groceries. He put the kettle on for tea. He was in constant motion.

"There are many things to do. I want to get a stone for Juan. It's about $200. My friend, Ray, said he would drive me to see Juan's grave."

Kachin asked if she could join them.

"Of course," Michael said. "Maybe Kathleen would go, too, and say another prayer."

Later in the day Sister Kathleen went to the apartment to give Michael communion. He greeted her with a big smile, "Heard you've been giving safe sex lectures, Kathleen."

Kathleen blushed. "You heard about that, too, huh?"

"Yes, and I'm very proud of you. Just imagine, because of you there will not be one banana in the entire city that will catch AIDS."

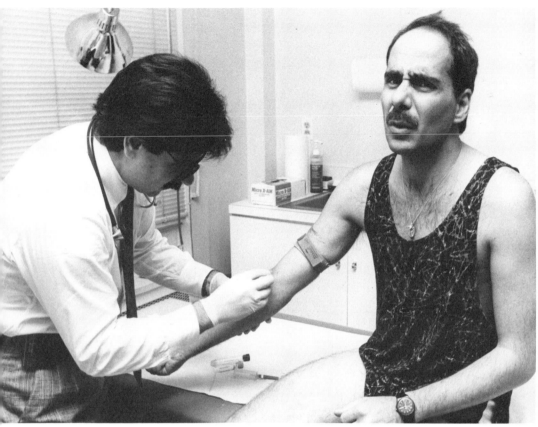

Dr. Wallach and Michael

Michael was getting better and better. He told Kathleen it was not necessary for her to give him communion at home. "That's the most wonderful news," she said. No longer reluctant to display physical affection, she hugged him firmly.

"I appreciate what you've done for me all these weeks," he said, still in her arms, "and now I would like to use my experience to help others. It's my turn to help." Kathleen was elated. She thought back to those terrible days not long ago when Michael was in the hospital. What a difference there was now.

Kathleen was setting up an outreach program at her church for people with AIDS. Michael agreed to be her guest speaker.

The first thing Michael did the following morning was to go to the

Montana/Wallach office in Greenwich Village for his biweekly checkup. He knew he needn't have breakfast because Renate, the medical receptionist, would have already ordered coffee and muffins for everyone. Somehow she knew how Michael took his coffee—light with sugar—and what kind of muffin he preferred—bran, lots of butter. Renate, working on at least five things at once while chatting with patients in the waiting room, provided reassurance for Michael and others. She was part of his reason for looking forward to visits to the office. Dr. Wallach greeted him in the waiting room, "You look terrific." Michael told him he never felt better.

Once inside the examining room, Michael coached the doctor through the exam. Dr. Wallach joked as he worked, "Michael, you can do this whole exam yourself."

"Don't I know it."

Not everyone can tolerate AZT, but weight gain and feeling well are indications of the drug's effectiveness because the patient's energy level increases and he is able to resume eating normally. Michael was one of the lucky ones who responded well.

The examination ended with an excellent report for Michael. He told his doctor that he was thinking about going to Italy.

"Bon voyage," Wallach answered.

Michael couldn't believe his ears. "You mean I can go?"

"Why not?" said the doctor as he washed up.

Michael sat thinking on the examination table for some time. Italy!

Dr. Montana

11 · DOCTORS

If Jeffery Wallach could have tolerated the long hours and early alarm clocks, he would have become a surgeon. Surgery is very satisfying—an open and shut case.

Infectious diseases was another branch of medicine where the patient was very often cured quickly. That seemed the kind of medicine he wanted to practice.

Following his internship, Wallach landed a fellowship at Cabrini Medical Center in New York City. The first year he was there about six AIDS patients showed up. "Quite honestly, if I had known what I was going to be dealing with, I would not have chosen this field of medicine."

Dr. Wallach's partner, John Montana, also got into AIDS by accident. He thought that he would be working with Hepatitis B, a deadly form of hepatitis that mainly struck gay men. A vaccine was finally introduced that was going to save everybody. As a physician serving the gay community, he was excited to be on the cusp of a real success story that affected his community. Then, AIDS hit!

Not only were the doctors frustrated by the lack of a cure for AIDS, they couldn't even control it. Finally, AZT helped some people with AIDS, but not all.

As Wallach sees it, AIDS would be the perfect virus for biological warfare, if it took effect more quickly. "It's a war. That's what it is," he says.

Drs. Wallach and Montana lose an AIDS patient just about every day. It is frustrating, sad, and frightening for them. "These are honest, hard-working, decent people," says Wallach. "Nobody deserves a disease. To see these people suffer is terrible."

The doctors and staff become unusually close to the patients, if for no other reason than they see so much of them. Dr. Montana says, "The hardest part is to watch someone we've befriended go from a healthy state to death. It's brutal. How can it not brutalize us?"

Each morning the two doctors return to their office after making hospital rounds and tell their medical receptionist, Renate, that so-and-so has died. They have no time to grieve for those who have died because there are so many living patients needing their attention. At some point, Renate says, each of them must deal with the horror of it all. For her it is often in her dreams—bad dreams.

The doctors and office staff watch out for one another. If one person is particularly upset over the death of a favorite patient, a colleague picks up the slack. Everyone in the office at some time has to shut the door and cry.

There are times, though, when they are able to bring about a big change in a patient. Dr. Wallach had a patient over the summer who was in intensive care. When both his lungs collapsed, almost everyone gave him up for dead, but Wallach and his patient's lover and sister worked with him around the clock for days. A lung specialist was brought in; in fact, every specialist Dr. Wallach could think of was called in on the case. To everyone's astonishment and delight, the patient recovered. "He is healthy—for now," says Dr. Wallach. "I don't know how long that will last, but when I see him come through the door of the office, I think to myself, if there was one good thing that I was able to do this summer, it was that. This man made the most startling recovery I had ever seen. If I can add even a month of quality life to one of my patients, that's thirty days worth of living and that makes my work rewarding."

The doctors feel they are getting more adept at handling the infections that regularly occur with AIDS. In the beginning they didn't know how to treat some of the opportunistic infections. Now they are learning. Also, the patients are becoming medically vigilant themselves. When their lungs do not feel right or they see a spot on their body, they call. That helps the doctors enormously. "Michael, for example, handles his illness in an exemplary way," says Wallach. "Oh, was he sick when he was in the hospital. When I see him now, healthy and energetic, I get chills."

Dr. Wallach knows that by taking the proper precautions, there is no danger in treating patients with AIDS, but it's something he thinks about. For the most part, no special precautions need be taken. If a patient comes in with open skin wounds, Dr. Wallach wears latex gloves throughout the examination, though he hates the feel of them. Before handling any kind of bodily secretions, such as blood, feces, urine, or sputum, he puts on the gloves.

The doctor does not wear a mask unless he feels *he* has something he might communicate to his patient. "I can't really imagine this virus is transmitted via tears or saliva. If someone salivated into a wound in your hand, I suppose the virus could be transmitted that way. However, the likelihood of that happening is very slim. I just wash my hands regularly."

Both doctors seek to give their patients as much control over their illness as possible. Some people want to know everything about their diagnosis, while others do not. Dr. Wallach says, "You have to be honest when you are dealing with a disease that is potentially terminal. I've never hidden a diagnosis of AIDS. That's violating my contract with the patient. Yet, with certain patients, when I first tell them the diagnosis, I sometimes do not use the word AIDS. For some, it is clear that they don't want to hear the word. They don't want to know more than that their immune system is not what it should be. Gradually they can face up to the name, Acquired Immune Deficiency Syndrome, AIDS!

"Other patients say, 'Doc, I want to know if I have AIDS.' Then, if they do, I tell them straight out, yes, you do. My job as a physician, no matter if the prognosis is terminal, is to provide hope because there is hope. I don't know whether a patient might make a turnaround. We are dealing with young, strong bodies. There are choices to make. For example, a patient will come into our office knowing what he has and insist he will not take AZT. I try to educate him by explaining how it may be helpful. I tell him we can start out on a low dose and see what it does. Nevertheless, I would never refuse to treat anyone who has his own ideas.

"The virus is less active when stress is eliminated. It's important to keep the patients psychologically strong. Therefore any activity such as exercise, vitamin therapy, or medication may be very important to control this disease."

Dr. Wallach refuses to say AIDS is always terminal. "Statistics suggests it is universally fatal, but you know, we thought this about polio and other diseases. But for them, if the patient managed to survive long enough, a cure was eventually found."

AIDS has made a big impact on Wallach's approach to medicine. He says he still doesn't know what death is. He is afraid of it, but working with AIDS patients has changed his approach to the dying person.

"Before, I willed my patients to live. 'Come on . . . Fight for that breath. . . .' I would try anything. Now, when the end is clearly inevitable, I will just make the patient as comfortable as possible, if that's what he wants. A patient can be alert and aware up until death without being in pain. The transition from life to death should be as smooth as possible. But if the patient wants to fight, I will fight beside him until the very end."

12 · R.& R.

In order to see Michael these days you have to make an appointment way in advance. The Quakers provide meals for PWAs on Mondays, Tuesdays there's a dinner at St. Peter's Church, and the GMHC recreation center makes lunch Wednesdays and Thursdays. "The community meals provide a great way to meet people. They eliminate the first step of telling someone new that you have AIDS because everyone there has AIDS. We don't ask a new person about his job or the college he went to. We ask, 'Are you on AZT yet?'"

A top priority for Michael is to participate in research projects focused on AIDS. He's part of a study that is examining the effects of eating habits on HIV infections. GMHC is studying how people are dealing psychologically with AIDS. Michael has not said no to any study that might help others learn more about the illness.

The best part of Michael's day centers around the recreation center. At lunchtime there he prepares the salad. He makes sure everyone has enough to eat. He is part of the telephone team that calls PWAs monthly to ask how they are doing and if there is anything they need from GMHC. People appreciate his concern as much as the wealth of information he provides about the latest medical findings. Michael doesn't pretend to be a social worker or a therapist, but his high spirits set a good example for others.

"It's amazing how much loving and caring is going on. So many people

Michael's water color

are truly concerned. I see it at St. Peter's, at the recreation center, amongst all the volunteers. There's even a British woman who wants to start a group called 'Straight People Who Care.' That blows me away. I'm doing many things that I never did before. It's hard to believe, considering the situation, but I'm actually having fun."

When Michael sees someone unfamiliar come into the center, he can usually tell when it is a first visit. He makes a point of introducing himself, and takes the new person into the office to introduce the staff.

One thing Michael hates is for another PWA to ask how long he's been sick. He would rather be asked when he was diagnosed. "Thinking of yourself as sick reflects a negative attitude. I won't do this."

At one of the GMHC luncheons, Michael met a newcomer, called Julius (name and identity changed), who had everyone at the table hysterical with jokes and outrageous stories. Michael thought Julius had a sensational attitude and wished he could be funny like him.

The following week when Michael was covering the office for the staff, Julius walked in looking very depressed. "What's wrong?" Michael asked, "you don't look so good." Julius brushed it off as just feeling a little down. Michael asked him if he wanted to talk about it. Julius, surprised that anyone would want to listen to his problems, began to talk. Before long he was spilling out his guts. He said he hated his job as a messenger riding around the City all day. He worried about his health once the cold weather set in. There was not one thing in his life that he enjoyed doing, and worst of all, he knew he was going to be alone for the rest of his life.

"So what makes you think you're the only person who is going through this?" Michael asked.

Julius looked up. "Michael, you're not like me. Every time I see you, you're so up and so together." Michael was amazed to hear this because he had been thinking the same thing about Julius.

"You don't see me when I go home and close my door," Michael told him. "You don't know what I go through when I'm by myself. I'm lonely, too."

With that, Julius began to cry. Michael held him tightly. "You needn't be alone all your life. You may think you will be, but you don't have to be. You can start from scratch again. Get your act together. It's the quality of life that counts, and that depends upon the things you do, the people you're with. All the bullshit is out of my life. Now my life is the way it should have been all along."

Through his tears Julius murmured that his disability insurance had just come through. "So what are you crying for?" Michael said. "Doesn't that mean you can quit your job? You have a lot to look forward to. You can do something that you care about."

The next night Julius called Michael at home. He didn't want to trouble him, but he just needed to hear the sound of a friendly voice. Michael said, "We are all in this together. You could never trouble me."

Dr. Montana had urged Michael not to surround himself with AIDS, because it wouldn't be good for him. But Michael sees it differently. Other people with AIDS inspire him. "This disease has given me so much. Now I know what illness is all about and I know how to listen. I've learned about caring. Helping. Loving. That is what I do now. So do many others. It's too bad it took something like AIDS to do this."

13 · ANOTHER BUDDY MEETING

Beverly began the buddy reports with an account of Manuel's condition. Manuel was home from the hospital, weighing under 100 pounds. Beverly was continually amazed at his iron will to live. His lover, Richard, who had been so healthy, was not as fortunate. While Richard was in the hospital, his condition worsened and he suddenly died.

The day after Richard died, his family went to the apartment and found Manuel lying there, emaciated, in a hospital bed. Manuel was devastated by Richard's death. The apartment was in Richard's name only, and Beverly was concerned that Richard's family might throw Manuel out. Luckily, they were very decent about the situation and let him stay.

With Richard gone and Manuel's mother unable to speak English, Beverly was left with the main chores: prescriptions, conferences with doctors, banking, shopping, etc. She was worried whether Manuel could afford the rent by himself. Because he was so emotional, she was afraid to talk to him about money. Ernesto, the team's financial adviser, offered to go with her when she discussed it.

Beverly ended her report, as always, by indicating her respect for Manuel's unwavering dignity. Her relationship with him had become one of the most important in her life.

Sister Kathleen spoke next. Her client had been hospitalized. There were so many things wrong with him: TB, Kaposi's sarcoma, his immune system was completely shot. He was extremely depressed and would not

Sister Kathleen and her client

talk to anybody. No one thought he would come out of the hospital.

Then suddenly he rallied and returned home. He was eager to go outside and walk. Kathleen took him to his favorite restaurant for lunch. "He ate everything in the restaurant. He was so happy to be there. He's a very gentle soul. I hope he's okay," Kathleen said, knowing differently. She looked wistfully at the silent group.

Ed Hartmann, whose wicked humor never failed to relax the stressful reports, broke the silence. "My client was diagnosed four years ago. There are people who have lived longer than four years with AIDS, but he has had very, very serious illnesses. When I met Steven, he looked like he was on his way out. That was two years ago. He was very thin. He's had KS, CMV, MAI (tuberculosis of the bone marrow). He got transfusions for the MAI.

"Steven was convinced that because no one had donated blood in his name, the hospital was making him wait for his transfusions. Steven is not one to wait for anything. He got forty-two people to go and give blood for him. He said, 'You know it isn't easy to find forty-two. You can't just call up and ask.'

"He's too much. He's on all kinds of drugs and he still goes to work every day. He doesn't have to do anything else. People do things for him. It takes a lot of organization to get all his friends to do so many things for him and he loves to organize. He needs a switchboard next to the bed to handle all the phone calls.

"Steven's a walking encyclopedia on any condition related to AIDS. All kinds of people call him up and ask him questions. Steven's doctors don't know what to make of him. They pretty much do whatever he says at this point. They don't know why he is still alive. So don't get in line for his apartment."

Ed has breakfast with his client every Sunday morning. Then they do chores. He keeps track of Steven's medications. Last Sunday Ed pulled out everything that was over three months old, things that Steven had tried, but didn't like.

"I went through the house and emptied all the garbage. Then we went to the movies. It's a whole day."

Steven is starting to get KS lesions on his face. In Ed's experience that usually makes a person unwilling to go out and be seen in public. "But nothing stops Steven. He was showing his lesions to the waitress at breakfast."

Brooke cuts in. "He's the most incredible person I've ever met. He calls me now. I'm on his list."

"Oh? Well, he must consider you high risk because he didn't hit you for blood." Everyone is laughing.

Ed

Ed's Client, Steven

Steven was born and bred in New York City. Like many others he became involved in the whole sexual revolution of the seventies and had numerous sex partners. By night he was seen at the best bars—the "A" bars—and the most select discos, with the "hottest" men in New York. By day he went to work in the public school system as a Supervisor of Special Education. He was well known among his colleagues as a fighter for the rights of teachers and of other supervisors.

During a routine medical examination in 1982, Steven's doctor discovered that his T cells were unusually low. The following year he began to feel ill and then developed shingles. Shingles in a young gay man can be an indication of a damaged immune system.

In August of 1984, Steven noticed two spots on his ankle. He brushed them off as mosquito bites but his doctor knew better. It was Kaposi's sarcoma.

Steven tried every kind of treatment for AIDS. He participated in early studies of experimental drugs and he also became involved in spiritual approaches to the disease, including healing circles and crystals. He tried acupuncture and he went to see a guru who visited the United States once a year and later shipped him Indian medicines. Steven realized that those who involved themselves only with the spiritual approach to AIDS were dying. There had to be a balance, and he decided that medicine, first-rate medicine, was the answer.

At first he tried to hide his diagnosis from his colleagues, but eventually his condition became obvious, from his weight loss and absences from school. Finally that excruciatingly painful infection, cytomegalovirus, put him into the hospital for two weeks. When he returned to work, he had a catheter in his chest. Two months later he was back in the hospital with MAI, a form of TB. One drug that was introduced into his catheter to control the MAI changed the color of his skin. He labeled his new skin tone "the Bombay look."

Friends and colleagues rallied. They threw a black tie birthday party in his honor, in a loft in Soho. Guests were charged twenty-five dollars and the money was given to Steven in case he needed extras. One hundred people showed up. Many teachers began to give blood in his name, cook his meals after school, and make donations to AIDS research organizations.

When Steven could no longer take the strain of supervising numerous schools, he was reassigned to a new job at the central office. He made sure everyone in his office knew about him. "At first they were a little fearful, but as they got to know me, they got to love me." Steven is matter-of-fact about his effect on others.

Then the phone calls started: "Hello, I'm a teacher in Brooklyn. I have a brother with AIDS and I don't know what to do." "Hi, your name was given to me by so-and-so. I have been diagnosed. Can you help me?" "I'm a Principal in one of your schools. We have a teacher on staff who needs some counseling." Through networking, Steven became the person to call. "I became something like a cult figure," he reports.

After work each day, Steven goes home and hooks his permanent catheter to a plastic bag hanging from a hospital pole that holds his cytomegalovirus medication. Following this treatment, he takes an hour break before hooking himself up to another machine that regulates the flow of nutrients into his catheter for ten hours. AIDS is a wasting disease, and a person often continues to lose weight, thereby becoming more susceptible to infections. To guard against this, Steven pumps nutrients directly into his bloodstream. Ear plugs block out the machine's hum and allow him to sleep.

For a long time Steven's friends cooked all his meals. Because of his condition, he became eligible for a five-course gourmet meal, five days a week, provided by the volunteer organization called "God's Love, We Deliver." Now instead of cooking every meal, his friends and colleagues contribute to the organization the money they might have had to spend on food.

Twice a week, however, Ed Hartmann continues to cook. He also checks Steven's medication and rubs him down with creams as they banter. Steven describes them as two yentas with sharp tongues who love to dish. "Ed puts me in my place whenever I have to be put in my place which is quite a bit. I listen to Ed."

After working at the Board of Education for many years, Steven is due a large pension. He is leaving certain percentages of his money to his friends in his will. He tells them he is quite willing to change the designated percentages if he is displeased with them. "You didn't call me this week—two percent *down!*"

His friends find the way he holds his pension over them as a threat very funny. He keeps the pension business going because he believes it helps to laugh about things.

As long as Steven is not in pain, he's in high spirits. On days that he's bedridden, his mind races and he becomes anxious and frightened. "Work is crucial for my well-being because I'm too busy to think about AIDS. I'm out of the house, amongst the working, amongst the living."

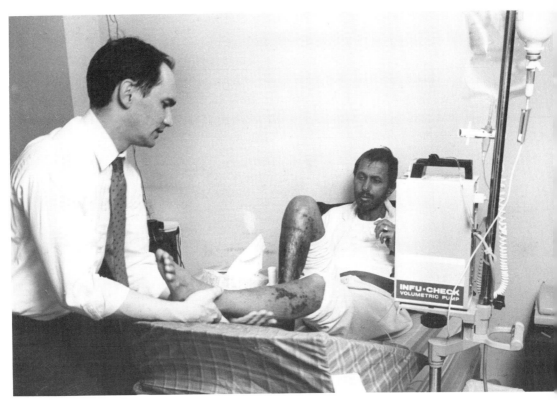

Ed and Steven

Lately Steven has been in good spirits because his heart and lungs are strong and he is not in pain. "When I see that I have survived this long, I think that I'll survive even longer."

In the four years Ed has been a buddy, he had sixteen clients before Steven. The longest lived for five months. He has worked with Steven for a year and a half. "With improved medical treatments, what will we do for people who live forever this way? What becomes our role? Are we going to become someone's housekeeper? I have been thinking about this because Steven has no intention of going away."

Brooke said, "It's a whole different ballgame from when I began this work." Her original impulse for volunteering was to help those who were alone and rejected, because she believed that nobody should die alone.

"The purpose of the volunteer program when AIDS first came on the scene was to help those who were deserted by everyone they knew, even by those in the gay community. We were there to develop a relationship, and getting groceries was a way of starting a conversation. That was why GMHC called the volunteers buddies and not housekeepers."

Dave Fisher's activities with his client included going to Broadway shows and apple-picking in the country. That wasn't what he had in mind when he signed up. He imagined the work would be exclusively around hospitals and sickbeds.

James Baggett had become so close to his client, Jon, that he dreaded the time when Jon would get sick. He was afraid Jon might become reluctant to turn to him in an emergency because of their friendship.

Ed understood James's apprehension. He said, "Even Steven, who has tons of friends, talks to me about things he doesn't want to talk to anybody else about. Death is too heavy a subject to lay on his friends and family. Last Sunday we tried to figure out how he was going to tell his Orthodox Jewish family that he wanted a wake with lots of flowers, like all his friends."

"That's ironic," said Kathleen, "my PWA wants a brunch."

"Unfortunately," Brooke said, "there is a down side to this increased longevity. The more you get to know somebody, the more attached you become, and the harder it is when they die. In the old situation, when somebody was desperately ill, you could keep a professional distance. When, over a period of a year, somebody is not getting sicker and not getting better, and you're still there for them, the relationship changes considerably."

Dave enjoyed being his client's friend, but he didn't think he was doing anything for him except being his *friend*. Kathleen replied that Dave couldn't do any more.

After much discussion about how to best deal with their jobs, the group decided to cluster their clients. Two or three buddies would share a few clients. In that way one person would not be left with all the physical chores as Beverly had been with Manuel. A second buddy would be there to share the emotional strain.

14 · MICHAEL

At three-thirty in the morning, Michael's alarm clock rang. He wanted to turn over and go back to sleep. Nevertheless, he knew the march on Washington for lesbian and gay rights was something he had to do.

He got up, dressed in layers of clothing, and packed a few containers of fruit juice and a sandwich into his canvas shoulder bag.

At four-thirty, Kachin, bleary-eyed, arrived at Michael's apartment. It was cold and raining.

Their first stop was the cash machine to pick up some money, and their second stop the grocery store to buy film, containers of coffee, and an apple turnover.

They took a taxi through the quiet streets to the GMHC headquarters. They wondered if anybody would show up. As the cab turned a corner, they saw two hundred people waiting to climb into four parked buses.

People were chatting with each other as the day trip began. They displayed home-made banners to wave at the demonstration.

Michael couldn't figure out why he felt as anxious as he did. Tears filled his eyes as he gazed out the window. He thought of Juan. Michael felt that he was marching for Juan. He had to be part of the march for everyone who had died of AIDS and for everyone who is going to die.

Kachin's straight friends were surprised she was marching in a gay parade. "Why don't people understand?" she asks. "You don't have to have AIDS, be gay, or a member of a minority to care about human rights. I'm not a good speaker or an organizer, but marching is one thing that I can do."

The sun came out as the bus pulled into a stadium in Washington. Everyone got out and took a subway to the Capitol.

The first thing Michael wanted to do was find the Names Project, the memorial to men, women, and children who died of AIDS. It is a quilt made up of hand-made panels, three feet by six feet, each one sewn in memory of a loved one. The panels were sent to San Francisco from all over the country by the friends, family, or lovers of the people who died.

In San Francisco volunteers sewed each panel into sections. There were twenty-four panels to a section. Walkways were sewn around each section that formed the huge quilt. At present the quilt is the size of two football fields.

Erwin, Juan's first buddy, had made a panel for Juan. Michael didn't understand why it was that important to see a piece of cloth with Juan's name on it, but he knew he had to do it.

Michael and Kachin arrived at the mall to find the enormous quilt stretched out. As they walked through the quilt, mothers, fathers, sisters, brothers, friends, and lovers stood before various squares, crying. The quilt was alive with color. Every piece made an individual statement. Some included personal poems. A favorite shirt or teddy bear were sewn onto others.

A friend said to Michael that quilts are made to protect you and keep you warm. The people memorialized in this quilt would never be cold again. They would always be protected.

Michael says, "I think it's the most unusual memorial in existence. Others are made of cold stone. This one is warm, alive."

Michael searched for Erwin's panel to Juan. Ushers were handing out programs that looked like a map. The names of each person with a square were listed in alphabetical order, and beside the names were the designation where their banner could be found: "L-1, L-2."

When Michael couldn't find Juan's name on the program, he went to the information desk and said he knew the banner had been sent in.

Eventually he learned that Juan's panel arrived late and did not make it into the quilt. All the pieces that arrived too late were left in San Francisco,

Michael

and were videotaped. A TV was set up on the mall to show the video.

There was a list of the two thousand people whose panels had not yet been sewn into the quilt. Michael spotted Juan's name. It stunned him. He turned and walked away. Then he went to Kachin, hugged her, and wept. Michael couldn't tear himself away from the quilt. For two hours he and Kachin sat, arm and arm, on a grassy hill and stared at it.

The march began in a vast field. Michael and Kachin wanted to march at the front of the line reserved for those who had AIDS. There were so many people milling about that they couldn't find the front, so they decided to stay at one spot and wait until a group they knew went by.

Behind street-wide banners groups and organizations from various states, churches, and schools marched by. Every gay activist and social organization was there from "Lesbians for Mao" to "Gays Without Dates."

Michael and Kachin looked for "ACT UP," an AIDS activist group. Michael says, "They don't sit back, they act, and that's why I want to march with them." Their banner carried Michael's favorite slogan, Silence = Death. The day before, Joe Dolce had told Kachin to look for him in the ACT UP group.

Michael and Kachin couldn't find Joe or ACT UP. When the GMHC banner came by, the two joined in. Michael says, "I was proud."

They saw many people they knew. As Michael walked along, he noticed John Montana on the sidelines taking photographs. He ran over and gave the doctor a huge hug.

In front of the Capitol was a stage set up for speeches. The march was so big that when Michael and Kachin arrived at the stage, the politicians, civil-rights leaders, and movie stars had already spoken.

By the time the march ended, the weather had turned cold again. After a quick lunch and visit to a museum, Michael and Kachin returned to the bus to begin the five-hour ride home. Michael says, "During the ride home I learned all about Kachin, her family, and her traditional childhood in Japan. Half the time we were having a pleasant conversation and the rest of the time I was teary."

Michael hurried back to his apartment and turned on the TV to see if the march was covered by the news. It was on for about thirty seconds. Thirty seconds of television coverage after what they had been through this day, what they'd gone through these years. Although he didn't expect any more from the media, he was angry.

Michael switched off his set, undressed, and got into bed. Lying there he thought to himself that it was time to leave Juan's death behind. Now he must remember the good times they shared and not dwell on his dying.

He held his favorite photograph of Juan, smiling in his Met's baseball cap, to his lips. He told the photograph all about the day he had had. He told it how much he missed Juan, that he still loved him, and nobody could ever replace him. Michael put the photograph back on the table by his bed, turned off the light, cried, and went to sleep.

GLOSSARY

AIDS COALITION TO UNLEASH POWER (ACT UP): a political activist organization set up to increase public awareness about issues involved with people with AIDS or ARC.

ACQUIRED IMMUNE DEFICIENCY SYNDROME (AIDS): is a still incompletely characterized infectious, transmissible disease in which the body's immune system is damaged in varying, often progressive, degrees of severity. As a result, persons with what many clinicians call frank, or full-blown AIDS are vulnerable to a number of serious, often fatal secondary or opportunistic infections and malignancies. (From *Medical Answers about AIDS,* published by Gay Men's Health Crisis, New York.)

ANTIBODY: a protein that the white blood cells make to fight infection.

AIDS-RELATED COMPLEX (ARC): early stages of the infection that fall short of meeting the criteria of AIDS. A person can show symptoms of having both diseases, such as fevers, night sweats, chills, and minor infections, but in order to have AIDS he must have an opportunistic infection.

AZIDOTHYMIDINE (AZT): an antiviral drug that has had some effect in slowing down the AIDS virus. There are many possible side effects, such as fevers, severe anemia which leads to bone marrow suppression, abdominal pain.

BUDDY: a volunteer who does day-to-day chores for a PWA such as buy groceries, do light housework, and take the client to the doctor. Basically he or she helps the PWAs gain control of their lives.

CLIENT: a PWA assigned to a buddy.

CRISIS INTERVENTION WORKER (CIW): a person who volunteers to work with a client, usually on a short-term basis, to help remedy an emergency situation. Often a client who does not need a buddy on a full-time basis will utilize the services of a CIW whom they can call upon to help out with a given problem: financial, legal, or emotional. The CIWs will also bring in an ombudsman when there is a hospital problem.

CRYPTOCOCCOSIS: an opportunistic fungal infection in the central nervous system.

CYTOMEGALOVIRUS (CMV): a virus related to herpes, which is an opportunistic infection in AIDS patients.

DEMENTIA: a state of mental disorder characterized by impairment or loss of the mental powers.

GAY MEN'S HEALTH CRISIS (GMHC): the first organization to recognize and confront the emergency of the AIDS epidemic and all its medical and psychological implications. GMHC has taken a leading role in providing extensive client support services, in educating health professionals, the general public, and high-risk populations, and in promoting funding for biomedical research. (GMHC Volunteer Manual, 1986)

GOD'S LOVE, WE DELIVER: a volunteer organization located in Manhattan, the Bronx, and Brooklyn, that delivers five-course gourmet meals to homebound people with AIDS.

HUMAN IMMUNOVIRUS (HIV): a retrovirus that selectively destroys T-4 cells. If there is a foreign body in your system, T-4 cells are activated.

HIV lowers or destroys the T-4 cells by entering them, multiplying once inside, and finally destroying them.

HYPERTHERMIA: abnormally high fever.

IMMUNE SYSTEM: B cells and T cells that distinguish between "self" and foreign chemicals and defend the body from invading microbes and cancer.

KAPOSI'S SARCOMA: a slowly spreading blood cancer which causes skin lesions, usually beginning on the back or the extremities as reddish blue or brownish soft nodules and tumors.

LYMPHOCYTES: specialized white blood cells involved in the immune response.

MYCOBACTERIUM AVIUM INTRACELLULARE (MAI): infections in the blood or other locations outside the lung. This bacterium, which is related to the organism that causes TB in humans, was rarely seen by physicians before the appearance of AIDS. People whose immune systems are intact do not get this form of TB.

OMBUDSMAN: an official who hears and investigates complaints by private citizens against other official or government agencies.

OPPORTUNISTIC INFECTION: an infection that takes advantage of a weakened defense system. The most common ones for people with AIDS are pneumocystis carinii pneumonia, toxoplasmosis, and cryptococcosis.

PENTAMIDINE: a drug used to treat pneumocystis carinii pneumonia.

PNEUMOCYSTIS CARINII PNEUMONIA (PCP): a type of pneumonia that is the most frequently diagnosed opportunistic infection in AIDS. People whose immune system is intact do not get this form of pneumonia.

PROTOZOAN ORGANISM: any of a large group of one-cell animals (protozoa) that include the amoeba and paramecium.

PWA: a person with AIDS.

PWARC: a person with ARC.

RETROVIRUS: a virus that contains RNA, which is used as a pattern for the cell to manufacture DNA (genes), which then directs the production of virus components.

T CELLS: a white blood cell lymphocyte that mediates cellular immune reaction.

T-4 CELLS: helper cells that coordinate the entire immune system to fight an infection. When a foreign body invades a person's system, T-4 cells are activated and coordinate the whole immune system to fight it.

T-8 CELLS: suppressor cells that subdue or stop the T-4 cells' immune response when the foreign body is no longer present.

TOXOPLASMOSIS: an opportunistic infection of the central nervous system.